Public Opinion in America

TRANSFORMING AMERICAN POLITICS

Lawrence C. Dodd, Series Editor

Dramatic changes in political institutions and behavior over the past three decades have underscored the dynamic nature of American politics, confronting political scientists with a new and pressing intellectual agenda. The pioneering work of early postwar scholars, while laying a firm empirical foundation for contemporary scholarship, failed to consider how American politics might change or recognize the forces that would make fundamental change inevitable. In reassessing the static interpretations fostered by these classic studies, political scientists are now examining the underlying dynamics that generate transformational change.

Transforming American Politics brings together texts and monographs that address four closely related aspects of change. A first concern is documenting and explaining recent changes in American politics—in institutions, processes, behavior, and policymaking. A second is reinterpreting classic studies and theories to provide a more accurate perspective on postwar politics. The series looks at historical change to identify recurring patterns of political transformation within and across the distinctive eras of American politics. Last and perhaps most important, the series presents new theories and interpretations that explain the dynamic processes at work and thus clarify the direction of contemporary politics. All of the books focus on the central theme of transformation—transformation in both the conduct of American politics and in the way we study and understand its many aspects.

BOOKS IN THIS SERIES

Public Opinion in America, Second Edition, James A. Stimson

Still Seeing Red, John Kenneth White

Governance and the Changing American States, David M. Hedge

Masters of the House, Roger H. Davidson,
Susan Webb Hammond, and Raymond W. Smock

Governing Partners, Russell L. Hanson

Public Opinion in America

MOODS, CYCLES, AND SWINGS

Second Edition

James A. Stimson

University of North Carolina at Chapel Hill

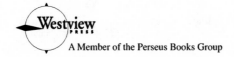

A Member of the Perseus Books Group

Transforming American Politics

Copyright © 1999 by Westview Press, A Member of the Perseus Books Group

Published in 1999 in the United States of America by Westview Press, 5500 Central Avenue, Boulder, Colorado 80301-2877, and in the United Kingdom by Westview Press, 12 Hid's Copse Road, Cumnor Hill, Oxford OX2 9JJ

Library of Congress Cataloging-in-Publication Data
Stimson, James A.
  Public opinion in America : moods, cycles, and swings / James A.
Stimson. — 2nd ed.
    p.   cm. — (Transforming American politics)
  Includes bibliographical references and index.
  ISBN 0-8133-6679-8 (hardcover). — ISBN 0-8133-6890-1 (pbk.)
  1. Public opinion—United States.   2. United States—Social
conditions—1960-1980—Public opinion.   3. United States—Social
conditions—1980—Public opinion.   4. United States—Politics and
government—1945-1989—Public opinion.   I. Title.   II. Series.
HN90.P8S84   1999
303.3'8'0973—dc21   98-36784
                                                                                CIP

The paper used in this publication meets the requirements of the American National Standard for Permanence of Paper for Printed Library Materials Z39.48-1984.

10   9   8   7   6   5

To Dianne Stimson

Contents

Tables and Figures

Tables

Figures

The living impressions of a large number of people are to an immeasurable degree personal in each of them, and unmanageably complex in the mass. How then is any practical relationship established between what is in people's heads and what is out there beyond their ken in the environment? How in the language of Democratic theory, do great numbers of people feeling each so privately about so abstract a picture, develop a common will? How does a simple and constant idea emerge from this complex of variables? How are those things known as the Will of the People, or the National Purpose, or Public Opinion crystallized out of such fleeting and casual imagery? . . .

The working of the popular will, therefore, has always called for explanation . . . what Sir Robert Peel called "that great compound of folly, weakness, prejudice, wrong feeling, right feeling, obstinacy and newspaper paragraphs which is called public opinion." Others have concluded that since out of drift and incoherence, settled aims do appear, there must be a mysterious contrivance at work somewhere over and above the inhabitants of a nation. They invoke a collective soul, a national mind, a spirit of the age which imposes order upon random opinion.

—Walter Lippmann, *Public Opinion*, 1922

Preface to the Second Edition

The idea of electoral moods is old, older than can be traced. But the concept of *public policy mood* and its indicator were my own thing when I wrote the first edition of this book. I did not wish them to remain so, for that would have meant that scholars had ignored my attempts to make this idea part of political science and public commentary on politics. The effort—which was considerable—in bringing this thing to life would have been wasted if it had remained only my private possession. I am gratified that it did not.

The mood concept and indicator have become part of political science. Used first by friends and graduate students, then by others in the small set of scholars devoted to longitudinal research on American politics, the concept has worked its way ultimately into the hands of scholars I do not know, writing on topics beyond my knowledge.[1] It is not mine anymore.

Some of the new scholarship on mood is my own, written with co-authors Robert Erikson and Michael MacKuen. I correctly anticipated both that I would some day address the dynamic representation thesis and that it would take a while. The product (Stimson, MacKuen, and Erikson 1995) demonstrates that all elected organs of American government are highly responsive to changes of public mood—much more so than I would have anticipated, and I think much more so than is generally believed, and not only by cynical observers.[2] So the work is no longer "unfinished," as I asserted in the original Preface.

Between editions the research program of this book continued at the University of Minnesota and at the Center for Advanced Study in the Behavioral Sciences. Paul Kellstedt and later Larry Grossback assisted in the updating and data management processes that are essential to this ongoing endeavor. I have incurred debts in this second installment to the University of North Carolina at Chapel Hill, to its Institute for Research in the Social Sciences, to Leo Wiegman (executive editor for Westview Press), and to Russell Dean (for assistance in updating the many data displays in the book).

By far my greatest debt, and one for which it is no longer possible to express my gratitude, is to Robert H. Durr. Bob Durr joined this endeavor as the first edition was nearly completed. He essentially took over getting that manuscript to press and was instrumental in all the research that followed, particularly the "dynamic representation" work cited above. Beginning as a research assistant, he became a source of advice, a wonderful critic, and, most a all, a friend. His doctoral dissertation at the University of Iowa took up the problem of explaining the origins of mood, work later published in the leading journals of political science. Bob died of cancer in 1996, his tragically short career encapsulated between the two editions of this book. I wish it were not so.

James A. Stimson

Preface to the First Edition:
An Unfinished Essay?

Looking back, you could see it. For a period, roughly that of the Carter administration, it was afoot. A quiet rumble of change moved through public views of government. None of its pieces was a stunning reversal, none so unlikely as to signal much by itself. But one segment of the public and one issue at a time, the small changes back and forth started instead to be changes all in one direction.

Americans were beginning to turn away from the long-preferred solutions to public problems. They had called upon government to protect health and safety in the workplace, to defend the natural environment, to promote equity in social relations. They had been doing so in these and dozens of other areas for some time. The direction of change most of the time was toward more. And then in the late 1970s they began to want less.

You could see it in a tax revolt, rippling across the nation from a start in California. To pay less instead of more is of course the desire of all taxpayers always. But this revolt had a different feeling; it was angry, intense. It had more the feel of deadlock over cherished symbols than mere adjustment of state and local finance. You could sense that its angry leaders were disillusioned people, so accustomed to losing that they did not know how to react to success and were not ready for it when it came.

Deregulation was the great innovation in the national politics of the time. We reached the conclusion that government did too much. Whether to promote economic optimality or from anger at the beast itself, we came to view less government as the solution to problems of disparate industries, disparate areas of American life. "There ought to be a law against that," we had said for forty years. And then we had passed the law and enforced it. It was a habit of American life. Now we were reversing course, advocating fewer laws. We were advocating more freedom to do the things we had once, in the name of reform, restricted.

Like the states, we began to speak of massive cuts in the federal income tax. Proposals of increasing seriousness called for extraordinary cutbacks that were inconsistent with activist government, not cuts of a few billion dollars for fiscal stimulation, but cuts that would require the eventual unraveling of the welfare state. And the more serious advocates also wanted to index tax rates to inflation, a move aimed at permanently restricting the national government's revenue base. It would make the nation like many of the states, conservative in action (if not in preference) because it lacked the wherewithal to be anything else.

One could see each of these changes in view as separate. Each could be an aberration, each explainable as a discrete event in its own terms. But it was hard not to think something more general was going on, a change in national mood. Conservatism was waiting in the wings. It would peak with the ascent of Ronald Reagan, but it was under way before him. The signs now—if not quite so much then—are unmistakable. And Reagan's election would be one more change, explainable in its own terms, without recourse to shifting national mood.

In the long view this quiet rumble, this changing all in the same direction in one period, was not unique. Global reversals had happened before—and have already again. It had seemed the same in the late 1950s, but then it was a growth of liberalism, across-the-board changes toward preference for sharper, more powerful expansions of the national government. Then we wanted government to take a role in health care, to boost the quality of our schools, to bring equity to race relations. And again all these things could be seen as separate issues, but movement was in the same direction for all. Then, as in the late 1970s, it was a movement of frustration as the growing majorities for change saw no result. (That the procedural conservatism of American political institutions stymied liberal majorities was the theme of the "reform" literature of the time.) And then the dam burst and change came in a flood.

These stories of American public opinion are true to historical fact as I know it. But they are stories, narrative accounts that weave an interpretation around necessarily selected highlights. That is not what this book is to be. Instead, we need to go beyond selection and interpretation and try to deal with what public opinion was. We need to understand and then measure this thing in a way that doesn't float on casual opinions, that isn't dependent upon choice of interpretative framework. That is the focus of this book: developing the concept of mood[3] and then measuring it.

Why Unfinished?

Public opinion, like the stripes on the back of a snake, may be described for the pure curiosity of doing so. But pure curiosity doesn't take us far. We like to think that what we describe matters. Do the stripes make a different snake in some Darwinian sense? If so, then the stripes are more than description and those of us with no professional interest in herpetology may find our interest captured.

Public opinion too must matter if we are to regard it worth description. A story of public opinion as it influences grand movements of public policy is a better story than one of public opinion that influences only itself. It is the story I will someday tell, I hope. But that isn't the story of this book, because the telling requires a research enterprise of considerable scale. Movements in public policy must somehow be measured and on some scale meaningful over time. And then a link between public opinion and policy will be found. Or it won't be.

This book is an unfinished essay in the sense that the link of opinion to outcomes is not demonstrated here. Page and Shapiro (1983) draw it quite directly. Wright, Erikson, and McIver (1987) have similarly demonstrated a powerful link between public opinion and policy in state politics. And since at least James Madison, uncounted authors have been comfortable presuming that opinion has consequence for policy. The link is less than certain. But it is not controversial.

This book is unfinished because it is about public opinion only. Opinion, in the naive version of democratic theory embedded in the American culture, moves governments. In the early jargon of social science research it is the "independent variable."[4] It is the thing thought to move the other thing, policy. But to sustain an interest in the "stripes" of public opinion—which do, incidentally, look a bit like a snake's stripes when presented as time series—the reader will initially have to grant a *presumption* that opinion matters.

The book is about American politics because that is what I know and because the empirical materials have to come from some place. Handling this one case is quite enough work, if never enough generality. But there is a happy message in this essay. Public opinion is about as institution-free as anything in politics can be. And it is the specifics of political institutions that so restrict our ability to create theories of general interest.[5] The happy message, then, is that a model of public opinion that works for the American case ought to transfer across national boundaries with a minimum of difficulty. Its central presumptions, of people with attitudes toward public policies that might move in parallel over time, do not require a Congress or Supreme Court. Indeed, not even elections appear in the "finished" version of this unfinished model. The model ought to be applicable to, if different from, everything from town meetings to military dictatorships. There is nothing American about mood. There is nothing specific about it either.

Public opinion is usually pretty specific stuff. Respondents are questioned on issues arising in a single polity, and the questions themselves are often particularistic. That is unavoidable. Without sharp focus, respondents inattentive to political debate aren't likely to report much worth knowing about their attitudes. Thus, much of our literature on public opinion is particularistic, telling us, for instance, what proportion of respondents would permit legal abortions given specific circumstances of mother and fetus. The issues are specific and bound to place. Often too they are bound to time, a central problem to be confronted in this essay.

But necessary as it is, specificity leads us astray in public opinion work. It leads us constantly to presume that the attitudes we measure mean what the questions ask. Without it we ask questions that produce mush for response. With it we want to believe that the crisp response to sharply framed query is a response to the query itself. And so we catalog opinions according to questions that produced them and in the process forget that there might be something like public opinion (singular) that is far more powerful and far more interesting than the questions that are its indicators. That, at least, is the position I will take in this essay: that the good stuff is diffuse and global, not specific.

Political Science and Journalism

In American politics there are usually two views of the same public opinion. Journalists and commentators read the polls and make interpretations of what they mean. Opinion analysts of diverse disciplinary background—whom I'll call political scientists so I don't constantly repeat that phrase—read the same polls as well. And unlike the journalists' interpretation, ours is often quite circumscribed by distrust of the data that indicate change, the marginal totals. Because our interests lie elsewhere, the marginal totals are rarely more than a parameter that is useful leverage for a comparison. We don't often care much about the thing itself.

We coexist; the coexistence is increasingly a peaceful one. Political scientists often read journalistic interpretations of public opinion. Journalists occasionally read our work. Although journalistic practice is somewhat responsive to the more technical work on public opinion, usually the journalists don't find public opinion scholarship very interesting. The commentators focus on politics here and now. The scholars do not; our excursions into statistical models of decades-old data can be a source of amusement for our journalistic brethren.

There is some respect, back and forth. But we work by very different rules of relevance and evidence. Journalists who write about public opinion often spend a lot of time talking to politicians, themselves astute observers of public opinion. Probably that is a useful focus for their insights, for they get constant input on what is important. We don't talk to many politicians, and when we do our agenda isn't "What's happening now?"

Political scientists who write about public opinion are usually well informed about journalistic commentary. But though we know it, we don't address it in our work because journalism is not scholarship. What is widely believed by astute observers isn't a theory or empirical regularity in need of test. And this is no complaint. That is as it should be. The newspapers cannot set the agenda for scholarship.

Journalists pursue "news" as a criterion of relevance. Change is news. Stability isn't. Their bias is to see change and novelty that isn't there. Scholars pursue science as a criterion, which carries another bias altogether. We see the world through theories and models, and that which is not relevant to them we tend not to see at all. Our bias is not to see change and novelty that is really there.

The point to this digression is that journalists have long commented upon public moods and political eras. We political scientists rarely do: Empirical work on public opinion pretty much ignores such ideas.[6] Who is right: the gambling journalists who make much of slim evidence or the cautious political scientists who make little of much? Both—and neither. Journalists, particularly commentators, are more creative, focused on seeing the novelties of political life and bringing meaning to them. Moods and eras are old hat to them; they have seen it all before; they have said it all before. Scholars are more disciplined, and disciplined observation, almost by definition, is not creative. To date, that discipline has largely precluded observation of meaningful movement over the medium term.

I wrote this book, more than other works I have authored, with an intent that it be widely read. I have tried hard to speak to a sophisticated general reader, to break away from the special language of social science that is convenient within its fraternity but a barrier to those outside who prefer their native English. There are occasional points, such as the elections analyses of Chapter 5, where I have had to employ the scholarly toolkit. But I write knowing that those tools will be inaccessible to many readers who, if they are patient with me, will find that the whole message is in the text.

I have tried to limit citations to the scholarly literature. That is easy in part, because this aspect of public opinion, the evolution of general sets of beliefs and views over time, is little studied. But it is hard in part, because to avoid citation is to appropriate merely borrowed ideas for ourselves.

The Essay and the Unfinished Grand Design

The ultimate purpose of this research is the study of representation, specifically, longitudinal representation, or governments responding to shifting public mood. This essay is about public mood only; the representation study is under way as I write. But it is ambitious, and I am plodding. There is reason to expect that its product is some time off.

I have some remarks about public opinion that stand on their own. I have done a good deal of development of theory and operations. I have collected a great deal of public opinion data. And I am ready to turn my attention away from public opinion; that part of the work is near completion. This somewhat informal essay is a compromise. It is not the ultimate statement of how democratic politics works that I wish to make some day. But it is a statement of completed work that I can make now. And I write it now while it is fresh.

J. A. S.

NOTES

1. This process is aided by the public availability of the mood data (in both annual and quarterly versions) on my web site: http://www.unc.edu/~jstimson. I intend for it to remain available and expect to continue to update it for as far ahead as I can now see.

2. That work is extended in Erikson, MacKuen, and Stimson (n.d.) *The Macro Polity*, to be published by Cambridge University Press.

3. Mood as a global sentiment underlying public opinion is an old idea, if not an old scientific idea. My usage of it is most directly influenced by Kingdon's (1984) discussion of "national mood."

4. But in the better jargon of current social research, it quite probably is not "exogenous"—free from the causal influence of anything in the opinion-policy-outcome nexus.

5. This is a point all but unnoted in the newly popular focus on institutions as the central fact of political life. There was a reason the "old" institutionalism fell into disrepute; it was built on particulars, assertions about, for example, House procedures that did not generalize to Congress, let alone legislatures, let alone political decision-making bodies. The "new" institutionalism needs to be wary of the same trap.

6. But see Smith (1981, 1990).

Acknowledgments to the First Edition

The research program from which this book derives had its origin, as best I recall it, in a University of Iowa graduate seminar discussion of John Kingdon's *Agendas, Alternatives, and Public Policies.* My first debts therefore are to John for provoking the discussion and to the students in that seminar (in particular John Heraldson, Eduardo Magalhaes, Glenn Mitchell, Mark Somma, and Steve Nelson) for making it so interesting that I could not put it aside and go on to the next topic. The work proceeded, more or less underground, for two years. During that time virtually everything in the project was tried out on Chris Wlezien, whose critical enthusiasm left its mark.

My largest debt for monetary support is to the National Science Foundation, which funded this research in grant SES-9011807, "Political Eras and Representation." Support by the University of Iowa's Bose Endowment was particularly helpful in the earlier, more playful, stages of the research program. An early public presentation, sponsored by Larry Dodd's American Politics Institute of the University of Colorado, Boulder, was a spur to development. Once formally and more often over food and drink, the work was presented to and tried out on members of the Political Methodology Society at summer gatherings. Among many who contributed something, Neal Beck, Henry Brady, Gary King, Bill Flanigan, and John Freeman left a significant stamp. I am particularly indebted to Chris Achen, who not only suggested the regression estimator I develop in Chapter 3 but also worked through its properties in several lengthy and helpful communications.

Jennifer Knerr, Mike MacKuen, and Tom Smith have been through every page of the manuscript, and all have kept me busy trying to live up to their standards of quality. I fear that I have not done so, but I know their comments moved me in the right direction. MacKuen and Bob Erikson, collaborators in an undertaking to attempt a comprehensive macro formulation of American politics (of which this work should one day be part), have been looking over my shoulder on this for three years. Others who have read, discussed, or criticized pieces of earlier work include Bruce Oppenheimer, Richard Waterman, Kathleen Knight, Carolyn Lewis, Jack Wright, Pev Squire, Cary Covington, Bob Boynton, John

Nelson, Tim Hagle, Art Miller, Lee Epstein, Richard Fenno, Heinz Eulau, Dennis Chong, Ted Carmines, John McIver, Richard Sobel, Warren Miller, and Rick Lau. For a project of short duration (by my plodding standards), quite a number of graduate and undergraduate assistants have contributed their ideas and labors. These include John Heraldson, Glenn Mitchell, Fred Slocum, Suzie Deboef, Bob Durr, Paul Kellstedt, and Barbara Allmart of the University of Iowa and Tami Buhr of Harvard University.

Acquiring public opinion marginals I found is no easy matter. They are all over the place, but one needs to know where to look. Robert Shapiro of Columbia University is a master of the search. I am greatly indebted to him for patiently teaching me how it is done. And often the search was unnecessary because he (and varied coauthors) had already done it so well. Kelly Patterson and Laura Crockett helped to make that knowledge sharing possible. The Roper Center for Public Opinion Research of the University of Connecticut is a principal data source for this research. Marilyn Potter and others of the Roper Center staff have been consistently helpful. National Election Study data were provided by the Inter-university Consortium for Political and Social Research.

And not by any means least, my thanks go to Larry Dodd for talking me into this project in the first place. Larry, as series editor, and Jennifer Knerr, acquisitions editor for Westview Press, proposed the idea of an extended essay that was the origin of this book.

J.A.S., August 1990

Public Opinion in America

1

Public *Opinion?*

People in and around government sense a national mood. They are comfortable discussing its content, and believe they know when the mood shifts. The idea goes by different names. . . . But common to all . . . is the notion that a rather large number of people out in the country are thinking along certain common lines, that this national mood changes from one time to another in discernable ways, and that these changes in mood or climate have important impacts on policy agendas and policy outcomes.

—John W. Kingdon, *Agendas, Alternatives, and Public Policies*

People think about politics. Not often. Not systematically. But they do. Ordinary people do. People, as we say, "on the street," have views on public affairs. They have concerns about the public order. Sometimes this means the public order only insofar as it affects their lives. But not always. They have ideas of good and bad, of progress and regress. They see the results of government, liking some, disliking others. They connect them, loosely to be sure, to policies. And they come to have views about policies, what works, what doesn't, what we need more of, what less. This is public opinion.

Usually we overestimate how often people think about politics, how much they care, how thoroughly they see connections between choices and consequences. That, in any case, is our past. Two generations of public opinion scholarship is a corrective, painting a portrait of ordinary people who don't know much, don't care much, don't know or care often. That corrective was sorely needed, for the original views flowed more from normative tilts toward what citizens ought to be than from what they were. For two centuries we tried to see people as democratic theories said they ought to be. And while we did, we didn't see them as they were.

But the corrective too needs correction. We found that citizens were often not philosophers of the public order. And in finding that, we built a vision of the contrary, citizens as dolts. We imposed models of the informed and thoughtful citizen on the ordinary men and women we

1

studied. They did not measure up. They did not come close to measuring up. Their ideas seemed ill formed, casually taken up, casually discarded. When we sought structure in individual attitudes, we found instead disorder. We were unprepared to be told that ordinary people didn't care very much about public life. They told us that they didn't know very much. And they didn't seem to mind not knowing. The topic didn't seem to be worth mastery.

What we found is that citizens, taken one at a time and in the norm, did not seem to be competent by the standards of democratic theory.[1] They could not act as individuals in the prescribed manner. And that may well be true. But should we take them *one at a time?* Is that the nature of politics? Or is public life instead the life of the herd? We carry normative blinders about this issue. Terms like *herd* or *groupthink* express them. We like individuals, distrust aggregations. But one of the plainer facts of everyday life is that individuals do not function as individuals. They are enmeshed in a social environment. They interact. They give, receive, borrow, and steal things from one another. Some of those things are ideas. Some ideas are about politics.

We corner individuals in their living rooms or on their telephones, all by themselves, for a survey. And we come to think of them as individuals, "the respondent." But "the respondent" is an abstraction of a real person, normally *not* by himself or herself, whose ideas come only partly—and maybe in pretty small measure—from self. We forget that we are interviewing not a self-contained individual but a spokesperson for the herd. And because ideas are borrowed from the social context, the specific elements of them may be borrowed without much supporting structure.

If our topic is people, then this abstraction as individuals is relatively harmless. If we want to know how people think, then perhaps an order and harmony not of their own creation may be omitted. But if the topic is politics, then it matters a great deal if aggregate opinions are more orderly and meaningful than individual ones. For it is the aggregate that matters in politics. To think otherwise is to confuse our normative preference for individualism with the reality of social order.

Social scientists commonly assert that individuals are real whereas aggregates are abstractions, created for convenience.[2] But except perhaps for hermits, there exist no atomistic individuals whose ideas or context of ideas are wholly their own. The individual too is an abstraction, a slice of the social pie temporarily considered as a unit. This view is so obviously true as to count as a platitude, but it goes against an extraordinary bias to the contrary deeply embedded in Western culture.

Considering the public nature of opinion holding helps explain why the pieces of opinions we get from individuals will sometimes seem so unrelated to one another. For the individual opinion holder they are unrelated.

If the structure of everyday views arises in part from interaction, then we would not expect to successfully recover much of it from individuals. But a more important implication is that we might expect to find structure in aggregates. Opinion, that is to say, may be meaningfully *public*.

This is not a new idea. We investigate aggregates all the time. We ask, for example, whether men (in the aggregate) have differing attitudes toward women's roles in society than do women (in the aggregate). Individual men and women are just respondents; it is aggregated men's and women's attitudes that answer the question asked. Focusing on national aggregates over time is not novel either. "Trends in public opinion" is a virtual cottage industry.[3]

What is different about this research program and this essay is the addition of a second level of aggregation, over issues. Just as respondents are mere units of analysis, the level at which measurement operations occur in typical public opinion work, here the questions themselves (the usual dependent variables) are mere indicators. Aggregating over people *and then* over issues to a single measure that varies only over time is the normal procedure of this essay.

The goal of all this aggregation is something deeper than mere response to survey items. It is the shared thing carried by individual people that underlies common response to disparate issues. It is latent, this thing to be called *policy mood*. Thus it can't just be asked, like a survey question, for most of us may not be particularly perceptive of subtle changes in what we think of and want from government.

On Politics at the Margin

The focus of this essay is change. But change of a kind that is not the routine stock in trade of political science. We tend most of the time to look for big changes. Because of the cross-sectional approach that dominates our thinking, we want changes to be so pronounced that they are in themselves "findings." And so our first inclination when we look at time series—collections of measures of the same thing at different times—of anything political is to look for *interventions*, points at which the differences before and after are so conspicuous that they can be argued to be important.

Public opinion time series sometimes exhibit such changes, but they are usually trivial. Big changes in public response are generally attributable to an event or shift in context that produces a notable difference in what the question *means*. Page and Shapiro (1989, 4:38–39), for example, report the dramatic move toward support of price controls—overwhelmingly the result of changes among Republicans—that followed Richard Nixon's 1971 imposition of controls. The explanation for the shift is too obvious to be interesting.

If not big changes, then what? The consistent viewpoint of this essay is that change that matters is change at the margin. The regularities of political life (and not just *political* life) are to be understood as responses at the margin to changes in the environment (such as public opinion) at the margin. Always looking for the bigger impacts simplifies design a bit, for they are easy to find. But if there are no big (and meaningful) changes to be found, and if the influence is still present, then we had better learn how to think about and model a world like the one of our everyday lives, where the constraints and parameters that matter vary in a narrow range.

To assert that change at the margin of public opinion drives politics is almost the same as asserting that public opinion is stable and predictable. For marginal change can be important change only when the underlying phenomenon is stable enough for marginal change to be noticeable change. The more stable a phenomenon, the more a marginal change in it alerts us to something important.

Is public opinion, and specifically preference for policy alternatives, stable and predictable? It often looks otherwise. We know, for example, that apparent inconsistency of policy preferences—the holding of mutually contrary views—is widespread. And Converse (1964) demonstrates widespread inconsistency for individuals over time as well. This suggests little stability or continuity. But public opinion in the aggregate is another story. There stability and predictability are easy to find, and when we don't find them it is often the case that "instability" arises from combining similar but not identical queries.[4] "Similar" won't do in time series, for the question-comparability effects—the differences in response produced by alteration of the wording of a question—are often larger than those representing real change.

If we collected series of identically phrased questions over time and asked how well a point in the series, say $t + 1$, could be forecast from knowledge available at t, the answer would be very well indeed. For comparable national samples of typical size, we could grow very wealthy by betting against all takers that the next value would be within a five-point range of the last. We would win more often than lose with a narrower, say three-point, range. The break-even point would probably fall within a range marginally less than two. Policy attitudes, correctly measured, are very stable. And when things that are stable change, even marginally, we are wise to take that change seriously.[5]

If we go looking for small changes that appear to have a cumulative character—I resist using the term *trends* for reasons that will later become clear—we can find them. They are there to be found. But cumulating change at the margin is of a smaller order of magnitude than the big interventions we usually seek. That is particularly the case when we concentrate on two time points rather than on whole series. It takes some discipline to turn away from looking for big effects, but the payoff is worth it: It allows us to see important patterns to which we are otherwise blind.

"Looking," "seeing," and "finding" will be common activities for the reader of this essay. For most of its evidence will be pictures, pictures of data where the reader can see patterns of change. And after our eye is accustomed to the year-to-year changes that signify little, we will look over and over for the more subtle, patterned movements. If the exercise is a success, that subtle change at the margin will come to seem inexorable, and we will come to see the year-to-year movements as noise imposed upon a signal. This essay is about the signal, the gradual movement of underlying sentiment, nowhere large and always dominant.

We are a bit like both tourists and geologists. As tourists we look at nature with a scale that appreciates mountains and seashores—big variations, easy to see. As geologists we look at the mere inches of displacement of adjacent land masses along a fault and infer the coming of earthquakes and volcanism. The two kinds of observation are of massively different scale. While looking at mountains, we can't see the inches that produced them and will create more. That requires looking away from the big and concentrating on the small but inexorable. That is the focus of this essay: finding movements of public opinion at the margin, movements that cumulate over time to produce a politics that changes remarkably, if not with quakelike suddenness.

It is not easy to see the subtle and inexorable in public opinion. Our traditions, both popular and scholarly, of thinking about what people want from governments are rooted in concern for the present, in "what's happening now." That usually leads us to think of levels of public opinion (does a majority support policy x?) instead of changes in it (is support up or down from last year?). And when we do think of change, it is often in the context of then and now; has it changed from some arbitrary time in the past to what it is close to today? Neither of those typical kinds of questions contemplates looking at change as a *process,* something that marches from here to there in increments, none impressive.

It is hard to see subtle movements, in part because only in the last two decades have we seriously gone about the business of producing the series of public opinion items that permit it. Those series will be seen to contain the necessary evidence. But it is easy not to notice it. And having noticed it, it is easy not to take it seriously. For how much can apparent patterns in one survey item mean? Even after we put aside the hobgoblin of sampling fluctuation, movements in support for a particular policy can always have explanations peculiar to the policy domain—and therefore not especially illuminating of a broader picture. If support for, say, federal government involvement in education goes up (or down), we can always conclude that it is the result of people's growing (or declining) concern about public schools. And hence our attitude toward the appearance of something systematic is "so what?"

"Old Politics," "New Politics"?

Discontinuity dominates our thinking about change. Our current events heritage and pretty frequent analysis of time series of two—then and now—usually leads us to look for sharp divisions between present and past. We have a considerable stock of theories and analyses based upon an assumption of a continuous, unchanging past, "old politics," somehow jolted into a new and discontinuous present, "new politics." If we then think of change as discontinuity, usually a single discontinuity, we naturally go looking for a single explanation for the single discontinuity. We ask why new politics is different from old politics, and the answer is a chorus: mass communications (by which most really mean television). "Then" we didn't have it; "now" we do. Although I do not wish to deny the genuine importance of mass communications for our politics, the point to be made here is that this style of analysis is singularly unhelpful for understanding political life.

"Then" and "now," with TV at the discontinuity between them, is too pat. Virtually beyond disconfirmation, this notion seems to explain things, and in the process prevents us from looking deeper. The problem here is not so much the single variable explanation as it is the starting conception of discontinuity. A pat question calls for a pat answer.

If discontinuity is the natural idea of change where longitudinal observation is primitive (and this may be a natural law), continuity is what we see when such observation becomes increasingly rich. If we observe almost any phenomenon at regular intervals over time, we will see change produced by the cumulation of small and irregular increments. If we do this for a while, look at many traces of many phenomena, the idea of change occurring as discontinuous jumps becomes increasingly an idea of oddball irregularities. Continuous change is ubiquitous. Things move. And that produces a revolution in our style of explanation. For continuous processes must drive continuous change. When something is happening all the time, one doesn't reach out for a single exceptional change as a worthy explanation. It doesn't fit.

If an aggregate time series moves between, say, 44 and 45 in successive years, we do not reach for an explanation of disorderly behavior; 44 to 45 requires no social calamity. "Then?" and "Now?" and "What is different about the two?" become silly questions when we are confronted with such continuous change. (And if we had observed only the two times, we would conclude conservatively, probably falsely, that *nothing* changed.)

Public opinion is no exception. Series of opinions, attitudes, and preferences, adequately measured over time, show continuous change. They move over time in irregular increments, no one of which typically is large enough to call for idiosyncratic explanation. Tested between one year and the next, the changes would only rarely be large enough to be statistically discernible. Looked at over the long haul, series that do *not* change are the rarities.

Continuous change that matters is usually cumulative. If movements too small to be discernible were also temporary, then their consequences would be too limited to merit much study. We end up studying problems that are instead cumulative (technically, "integrated"). Small changes become interesting when they add up over time to produce change of a scale that matters in the long haul. Most public opinion series have this character. They move up or down, left or right, irregularly over long spans of time—a movement captured better in decades than in years. Put another way, they do not equilibrate in the short term, throwing off deviations to left or right and always returning to some norm. Once moved, they tend to stay moved for a while, and that is why small movements matter.

If public opinion changes continuously, how and why and when it changes when it does is an explanatory problem of some interest. It is one I will nibble at in this essay and will make some progress on at the margin. But much more will remain unexplained than be conquered when I am done. This is not an easy problem. Its solution clearly will not come in terms of old politics and new, then and now.

Issue Opinions

Political scientists write of issues and mean one thing. Almost everybody else uses the word *issue* differently. At least since Stokes (1963) we have pretty much settled on the idea that an issue is a debate over public policy. Debates have two sides. A defining characteristic of the political issue, then, is that we must be able to imagine reasonable people advocating either side. Thus education spending is an issue; reasonable people can want more or less of it. "Education," though, is not an issue; virtually no one opposes it.

In popular commentary almost anything a politician says in a political campaign is called an "issue." Thus we have crime issues, flag issues, scandal issues, peace issues, and so forth. That usage isn't helpful, for it puts symbol and image manipulation, political rhetoric, into the same category as genuine political disagreement over what government ought to do. Stokes calls these image positions "valence" issues, as opposed to (real) position issues. Valence issues carry emotion and image but no public policy content. Emotion and image are real politics, often effective politics, but they aren't real debates over public policy. A George Bush visiting a flag factory in the 1988 campaign is wrapping himself in the positive valence of the national symbol; he is not raising a "flag issue."[6]

So too we need to split off claims about what has or has not been achieved from real issues. Peace and prosperity are outcomes, not debates. When parties claim to have done well managing the economy—or claim that the opposition has done badly—they are engaging in sensible politics. But this is no "economy issue." Issues are debates about valued alternatives. No party values hard times. Rarely does one value war over peace. Economy issues and war issues are possible, but they would involve debates about what ought to be done. Should we stimulate the economy to produce employment or does that raise too much danger of inflation? That is an issue. Reasonable people can take either side. Debates about whether things are going well or badly, in contrast, may be debates, but they aren't *issue* debates.

These distinctions are important because real issues behave much differently from valence issues or outcomes. The latter, particularly the valence issues, can be created and manipulated overnight. They can move from nonexistence to real political force in a matter of days. Real issues, representing hard choices between competing values, are stable. They are stable because they can't move without some cherished value giving ground. Valence issues have no such competition of values. A tug of war in which only one side is pulling is free to move a long way in a short time.

On Trends in Issue Opinion

Trend is a word that can be used seriously or casually. Casual use is the more common in discussions of public opinion. "What is the trend in attitudes toward handguns?" we ask, meaning, How have these attitudes changed the last two or three times they were measured? That is a harmless question, but it uses the idea of trend in a way that deprives it of a stronger meaning. The problem with the usage is that the only way an issue series can be said not to "trend" is to remain virtually constant. Any old movement becomes a trend.

Used more rigorously, trend is a powerful idea. And unless it is used rigorously its power is sapped by subjectivity; what looks like a trend to you may not to me, or vice versa. Before we ask, then, whether or not public opinion "trends" (or individual issues do), we need a rigorous definition of *trend*. The one I choose, drawn from the statistical literature on time series is this: A trend is a process that increments or decrements a series by a fixed amount at every interval. A trending series goes off in one direction, therefore, not for a while, but indefinitely. Regular increments at each point in time do not produce reversible processes; they go in one direction forever.

Many time series, including public opinion time series, appear to move systematically over time. The question of trend comes down to the issue of whether or not that movement is by regular increments. Because very large changes can occur by random processes, the common usage—how different a series is at one point compared to another—cannot be a test of trend. The test is whether or not that movement occurred in regular increments.[7] The common alternative, a series that moves substantially but not regularly, is called drift.[8] Most of what is called "trend" in discussions of public opinion is in fact drift, irregular movements up and down that lack the tendency to go off in one direction indefinitely.[9]

The point of a rigorous definition here is that it matters. In a short span of time trend and drift can look a lot alike. Over the long haul, which one it is, trend or drift, has prodigious consequences. Trending series go off indefinitely into the future always in one direction (which in survey marginals means that the item tends toward a state where one response option is chosen by all respondents and the question ceases to be asked). Drifting series, in contrast, lacking a unidirectional driving force, are likely to change course. After moving more or less in one direction for a while, they can turn and move more or less in the other.

It matters even more for theory. Trend requires explanation. If movement is always in one direction with some regularity, then something, some process, is driving that movement. Quite a number of social indicators are influenced, for example, by population size and so trend inexorably upward, as to date has the underlying driving force. Nothing "just trends" by some mysterious inner driving force. Trend requires process. Process requires explanation.

On Public Opinion Leadership

We are accustomed to seeing public opinion as scholars see it, as pollsters see it, as journalists see it, even to some degree as the public itself circularly views reports of its own views. I pursue here briefly the somewhat different issue of how elected politicians see it. I wish to suggest how it might matter. In particular I wish to suggest how it might matter without treating it only as a cause of electoral behavior. The view to be put forward is that public opinion matters and that most of what matters about it is not to be understood as a matter of votes and elections.

"People in and around government sense a national mood," repeating Kingdon's words from the outset of this chapter. "They . . . believe they know when the mood shifts." I consider the matter as a process and ask the motivating question: What would public opinion look like if you were an elected politician observing it? Where would you look for it? How, most particularly, would you come to know it? What would be the process of coming to know it, coming to be influenced by it?

I begin the answer to these queries with a postulate. It is unconventional, lacks anything like common agreement—some would probably say it lacks common sense. But I ask the reader's indulgence, because if it is seriously pursued, I think it has some power to illuminate. The postulate is this: Politicians engage in representative behavior because they wish to lead, to have influence on the direction of public opinion.

In the last decade or so we have become comfortable, too comfortable, I think, believing that we understood the central motivations of political life and that they were one, reelection. An interesting assumption in Mayhew's (1974) most influential work, reelection as central goal of political life seems subsequently to have been reified into a "finding." It has "everybody knows" status. A thousand times assumed, it has come to seem a fact. But it is not.

Reelection as central motivation was useful as an assumption; pursuing its implications led to insights. It is not useful as an accepted fact, for it has stopped us from asking the old question of why public officials do what they do. And it doesn't answer that question. It doesn't tell us why most people are not tempted by political careers but some are. It doesn't help explain why most of those who start down the path of electoral politics turn away after a brief experience but some stay on. Its implicit cynicism satisfies too easily our desire to know why people act as they do.

Elected politicians do, almost of necessity, desire reelection. Aside from those few[10] who have got themselves into a job they don't like, the lack of such motivation would be irrational. But the more important question is why they got into the job in the first place. We need to know what kinds of people put themselves in a position to *need* reelection and why they do so.

What makes politicians want to be politicians? What is unique about the political career? What aspect of a life in politics is more typical of politics than the alternatives the politician might have pursued? Power is usually the first answer to this query, but I don't think it is a very good one. For it overstates the power typical politicians—the 99-plus percent who are not presidents or U.S. senators and never will be—can reasonably hope to achieve. And then it compares the lives of politicians to the lives of ordinary people. But the people who pursue elective politics in the United States are in no sense ordinary. They are well-educated, talented, ambitious (often intensely so), hard-working people. Because of these attributes, they are the sorts of people likely to rise to the top in any career track, corporate, military, or whatever, where power accrues. It is a dubious proposition that relative success in politics offers more personal power than relative success in these other endeavors.[11]

Politics offers more limelight than many alternatives, it is true. If the corporate executive might have more real power to move people and material things, that power is much more private, much less visible, than say, that of the legislator. But in an era where seeking center stage *as a politician* also means seeking derision from a public that thinks badly of politicians, the limelight can easily be oversold.

Sometimes politics is said to appeal because it allows one to identify with the center of things, to be associated with the "action." Probably there is much truth in this answer as well, but it seems to me much more suited to explain the more limited involvement of amateur activists. The appeal of the action seems particularly strong for the political groupies always seen at party and campaign activities. The satisfaction of being able to say that one talks to "the senator" or some such claim would seem powerful enough to explain a few hours devoted to occasional political work but not enough for a lifetime choice.

Perhaps all of these explanations, each with some partial truth, together are enough to explain the choice of politics as a vocation. I am unconvinced of it. I think we need to look further, to find some satisfaction of the life of politics unavailable to any but politicians. Thus the postulate that leading public opinion is a central motivation for politics. Changing how the public feels about issues is something politicians can do. Indeed, it is something even fairly obscure politicians can do. Insofar as the elected politician is not wholly invisible, he or she can choose an issue, put a stamp of identity on it, and try to influence *public* response. The rest of us are limited to changing personal views, one at a time. This is a postulate, not an assertion of fact, because the only evidence I can offer for it is to say that it appeals to me. That is not evidence at all.

But grant me the postulate, for it has an implication I wish to pursue. If, in fact, politicians are seeking to influence public opinion, seeking to channel the stream, then it follows that they must stay in contact with it. It is ineffectual to stand outside the currents of values, preferences, and presuppositions and try to bend them to one's will. To be outside is to shout and not be listened to. The effective political rhetoric, in contrast, is to be able to say, "Listen, my values and preferences are like your values and preferences, and having looked carefully at this thing I have come to a conclusion that I know you would share if you did the same." Better yet is a public that *knows* it shares values with the politician. The politician with the most successful "home style" (Fenno 1978) is one whose public is so convinced that he or she shares their values that they become willing to assume the politician will do the right thing.

This value and preference sharing is good reelection politics. But it is also a near requisite for influencing public sentiment. If one's premises are suspect, all that follows from them is easily dismissed. The implication, one of some importance, I think, is that the politician who would influence the current of public sentiment must swim in it. What is shared between politician and public is rhetorical leverage to move those smaller pieces that are not shared. In order to lead public opinion the politician needs also to follow it, leading in particulars by following in general.

The significance of this view is that it predicts that politicians will flow with the moving current of public sentiment, a current that moves slowly, with some subtlety, back and forth, changing in tone and emphasis more than direction. And, importantly, this following of currents of public views occurs without invoking electoral sanction as cause. The politician of this account would do it for the positive goal of enhancing a particular kind of influence, not for the negative one of avoiding being one of the "rascals" to be thrown out.

Switching from liberal to conservative (or vice versa) or anything remotely like that is not in question. The behavior of following, I propose, is strategic and true to personal values. It involves lying low when views are out of favor, picking one's moments to step forward when it looks like they might prevail. But the aggregate result of these behaviors, if they follow the same public opinion signal, will look like movements from left to right or the reverse. For the aggregate will be the result both of numbers and of the volume with which they speak.[12]

We like to keep life simple by presuming that leading and following are mutually exclusive activities. And so in this simple view the politicians are either out in front (which gets our normative approval) or slavish followers, testing the direction of the winds (which we equally disapprove). Simplicity, when it works, is a powerful sword for understanding. I think it gets us into trouble here. Real-life politicians consistently resemble neither heroes nor fools. They are, rather, more prudent, occasional heroes but always calculating. They deal with risk, I think, as do rational investors, never fleeing from it entirely and always making certain that the risk premium—paid in influence—is worthy of it. And like rational investors, they must value good information. I turn next to the questions of where and how they get it.

Opinion Perception as Double Summation

If information about public views is vital and collecting it costly, how, we might ask, would a politician go about it? What would be the process of collection and storage? The political professional lives in an information-abundant environment. Information comes, often without being sought, from all directions. Politicians get information just as scholars do from secondary reports. They also get a good deal of information about the views of particular people on particular issues. But this latter information needs to be processed before it can be decision-relevant. The limitations are much the same as those of the survey researcher analyzing a single respondent. Without a wide range of information on the person's views, the researcher cannot interpret the particular bit at hand; it lacks the context of this issue as compared to others and this time as compared to last.

Useful, and therefore consequential, opinion is aggregate. Politicians care about the views of states, districts, areas, cities, what-have-you. Individual opinion is useful only as an indicator of the aggregate. For a politician to pay attention to individual views is to miss the main game; he or she is not a political scientist or social psychologist with an inherent concern for the individual. The politician must, as a matter of image, appear to be concerned about individuals, but aggregate opinion is what matters.

But even aggregated views will usually lack direct decision relevance. Politicians must deal with issues at a high level of specificity and then mainly with nonrecurring specifics. Public opinion is by necessity general, unfocused. Focus requires very high levels of decision-context information, too specialized ever to be found in the general public. That is a simple matter of division of labor. We the public are part-time players in this game.

The politician wishing to know public opinion for decisionmaking faces bad news. The information about public views is expensive to obtain, and even the most specific information one can have isn't specific enough for the decision at hand. Why pay the cost for specifics at all? I propose instead that a rational economizing collector of opinions would use that information to gain leverage on the evolution of public views at a very high level of generality, the level at which it is meaningful for a public mainly inattentive to public affairs.

If the issue at hand, for example, is how long the waiting period should be—seven days, thirty days, none?—for purchase of a particular class of handguns, the question is too focused, too specific, for us to have much hope of learning how the public will respond. The public doesn't have views at that level of specificity. When we encounter such specificity in survey data, for example, we would be most unwise to treat the answers as if they were as precise as the question. But such specific information clearly speaks to more general proclivities. Does the public want more or less regulation of guns? One can do reasonably well making inferences about the general from the specific.

Thus I propose an information-seeking and -storing process in which consequential opinion is also aggregated over similar issues. To know views on a very specific issue (e.g., what percentage supports a lengthy waiting period for handguns) is useful chiefly because it has implications for a set of related matters (e.g., other specific issues involving guns), which will be the direct subject of political action. It is unlikely that the specific issue (as stated, for example, in a survey question) will ever be directly the matter of decision and quite likely that some different, but related, issue will. Thus the primary information value of the datum is the generalization it permits.

The process may therefore be conceptualized as processing of information bits, where each bit, a datum, is made meaningful by aggregating over constituencies and over issue domains. For example, one sees a poll about how white New Yorkers feel about having a black next door. That is generalized to white New Yorkers' attitudes generally (summation 1) and racial policy generally (summation 2). The specific datum is useful mainly because it permits such generalization. Most of those who process the information will care neither about New York specifically nor about "moving next door" specifically. The datum is valuable as leverage on the larger mood, which the politician must know.

A third possible summation, over time, is different. We lose specific information when we sum over some dimension. Timeliness is often information we wish not to lose. In politics it is often critical to know what is current and not to confuse it with past or future. Thus we do not sum over time, because timing matters.

Public Opinion and Private Opinion

Public opinion as a topic is at least as old as democratic forms of governance. As a focus of systematic analysis, however, its origin is the origin of survey research on public opinion. Very early in this history scholars decided that the interesting questions that could be answered with the survey tool were about individuals, why one had views or behaviors different from another. That was the unique power and principal good of the survey design; it was a new opening into people's heads. Surveys could explain why attitudes developed as they did and how attitudes connected to behaviors, one person at a time. This was then an exciting new vista, the opening of the black box of individual political behavior. After years of frustrating speculation about why people did what they did, now we could *ask* them.

Scholarly analysis of "public opinion" became—and in general remains today—the analysis of *private* opinions about public affairs. This individual (or micro) focus leads naturally to public opinion as political psychology. Its focus on the individual actor raises many of the same issues as does psychology, and its tools, approaches, and concepts came to be dominated by those already developed in that discipline. "Public opinion," "political behavior," and "political psychology" could be quite different from one another but are virtually interchangeable in common usage. One could take a course with any of those titles and get the same materials. Much the same is true for the related area of voting behavior, also dominated by micro concepts and psychological analyses.[13]

The study of micro behavior is now a mature scientific subdiscipline. Its numerous practitioners operate with a high level of consensus about the basic questions to be investigated and the tools to be employed. Micro behavior may be considered a paradigm, in the sense of Kuhn (1962). It has all the requisites: leading theories, examples of success, focus on questions to be asked, and methods by which they are to be answered. Its growth changed the discipline from which it emerged, changed what it means to be a political scientist.

The success of this study of private opinions about public affairs may easily be understood as the result of scholars choosing to exploit what their tool, the sample survey, did well—and to ignore what it did not do well. One thing the survey does not do well at all is to inform us about *public* opinion. If one were to ask the proverbial man (or woman) on the street what was public opinion, he (or she) would be likely to define it in terms of what the public wants. And "the public" is singular. This is not a happy question for survey researchers, for their tool is not much use in answering the query. One can pose a query about public preferences on some issue and report the results—n percent favored x—but these marginal totals (or just "marginals") both lack interpretability and fail to exploit the power of the survey to discriminate between individuals.

The interpretability issue (to be taken up in more detail in Chapter 3), though simple to state, is not at all simple to solve. The problem is that the answers to survey questions are highly dependent upon what the questions ask, and we lack a scientific method for the design of survey questions. Survey designers do their best to pose queries that probe the concepts of interest, but their best is ad hoc and intuitive. Beginning students often see this issue as one of fairness or balance, of question designers slanting questions to produce the answers they want to see. It is much worse than that. The scholar pursuing objectivity, who just wants to see the world as it is, does not know how to ask the right question. Indeed, there is no right question.

This issue is under control in micro analysis, what I have called private opinion. There, whatever its unknown defects, the same question has been posed to all respondents equally. And so whatever "it" is, we can reasonably ask and answer questions about how individuals differ on "it." But there are as many public opinions on an issue as there are possible questions that might be posed, and, aside from those that show an obvious intent to produce one or another result, they are all about equally good. Thus, apart from some early excesses, reports of survey results are framed not as answers to "What does the public want?" but as answers to a specific survey question. We say, "To this question, n percent said so and so." We do not—cannot—say, "Public opinion on x is so and so." This is operationism, the defining of concepts in terms of the operations one conducts to measure them, in extreme form. We do it not because we approve of operationism, a naive view of science that forgets the role of theories and concepts in explanation, but because we have no choice.

But the person-on-the-street view of public opinion (as "what the public wants") has one considerable virtue: It is directly relevant to politics. It is the public opinion that matters. The irony here is that survey research, the tool that makes direct probing of public opinion possible, is the reason scholars turn away from its public aspect. The coming of the sample survey produced a political science rich in scholarship on micro public opinion, the analysis of individual attitudes and behaviors that deals almost not at all with the public.

Macro public opinion, or just *public* opinion, is the focus of this essay. Never much more complicated than "What does the public want?" it will exploit the fact of thousands of existing public opinion surveys, numerous samples and numerous items probed at numerous times, to lever meaning into each. The whole will be used to bring interpretive context to the parts, to extract real information from the marginal totals that cannot be had from one survey by itself.

On the Plan of the Essay

The design for this extended essay on public opinion is this: Chapter 2 introduces a series of ideas about how and why public opinion might move over time and how that movement might be related to what governments do. Chapter 3 attacks head-on the problems of analysis of the survey marginal to gain information about public preferences, ending in the development of a main measurement technology and some subsidiaries for cross-validation. Chapter 4 exploits that technology for description of policy moods, for cross-validating the measure, for comparison to a common alternative (self-declared ideological identification), and for a series of decompositions of mood into specific policy domains. Chapter 5 takes up the question whether policy mood influences elections and returns to an old familiar political theme, mandates. And last, in Chapter 6, the focus returns to American politics of the late 1990s and beyond as we develop the implications of what the measure seems to be saying about the current era.

The foundation for this whole scheme is a view of the structure—in particular, the structure over time—of public opinion and the place of public opinion in representation. That is the business of Chapter 2.

NOTES

1. These themes are clearly articulated in Berelson, Lazarsfeld, and McPhee (1954) and become central to the three-decades-old voting behavior research paradigm beginning with Campbell, Converse, Miller, and Stokes (1960).

2. This is most commonly seen in arguments about the "ecological fallacy" (Robinson 1950). See Erbring (1990) for a somewhat contrary view.

3. The numerous works of Robert Shapiro (see References) in *Public Opinion Quarterly* are outstanding examples. Smith (1981, 1990) takes up trends across (nearly) all issues in the postwar era.

4. Many of these points about stability and change in opinion series are similar to those of Page and Shapiro (1989), where they are more thoroughly developed in an entire chapter ("The Myth of Capricious Change") devoted to these issues.

5. This is often unappreciated because of a commonly held and fallacious understanding of sampling theory. It is commonplace to regard differences between independent samples of, say, three points as probably the result of random sampling fluctuation, because parameters from samples of typical size *could* vary about that much from chance fluctuation in about five out of every hundred cases. But that it *could* have occurred by chance with small probability does not mean that it is likely that it *did*. The misunderstanding is coming to believe that an improbable event, a difference so large that it could occur by chance only five out of a hundred tries, is likely. In fact, the sampling error with greatest likelihood is zero. And the range of values close to zero will represent most actual cases.

6. The flag desecration controversy was another story, but that debate arose from a Supreme Court decision issued after the 1988 campaign.

7. This definition has the virtue of an objective statistical test. In the common simple case, for the model $x_t = x_{t-1} + c + a_t$—in English, the series x at time t is a function of (1) its previous value, x_{t-1}, (2) a constant, c, added at every period, and (3) a random error component, a_t—whether the estimated value for c is statistically significant (whether, that is, we can conclude with some confidence that it is not zero) is a test for whether trend is present.

8. Yet a third alternative is simple random fluctuation—with or without ARMA (autoregressive-moving average) error aggregation processes (Box and Jenkins 1976)—around an equilibrium fixed over time. If that were the case, if public opinion were stationary over time, the only changes self-correcting random disturbances, then there would be no interesting variation to observe, and this essay would not be.

9. Smith (1981, 1990), for example, writes of a trend toward general liberalism in the postwar era that "plateaus" in the 1970s. The facts of his analysis are pretty much the same as my own to come. I do not disagree with his analysis; I just am urging a definition of *trend* that disallows the possibility of abatement or reversal. And, too, there is a difference of emphasis. Some issue domains, most notably racial and cultural matters, clearly produce liberal trends in the postwar era. A phenomenon of central import to Smith, these matters are peripheral in my analysis. It depends chiefly upon the focus. In the domain of culture and values, trends are abundant, perhaps normal (see table 4 in 1990:492). Attitudes toward religion, lifestyles, sex, gender, family, and the like—the "climate" in Davis and Smith

(1980)—show dramatic trending change. In the domain of public policy controversies—the "weather"—these critical social issues are but a very small part of the issue set and trend is the exception to the norm of cyclical fluctuation.

10. Whether it is few or many who desire the quickest exit from political life depends on what kind and level of politics we are considering. Barber's old (1965) but still up-to-date study of state legislators is a useful view of the other side of political life, a side where "going home" may often be the central motivation.

11. Financial gain used to be on the laundry list of motivations to public life, if never very prominently. The evidence now seems overwhelming that financial loss, relative to what could be had elsewhere by people of comparable talent and industry, is the more likely outcome of a political career.

12. This is similar in concept to the Converse, Clausen, and Miller (1965) assertion about the mass electorate that the apparent Goldwater surge in numbers of conservative voters in 1964 came largely from a small group who were very vocal. Were there a rich enough time dimension, I think we would have seen relatively constant numbers of such conservatives and strong variation in their frequency of public expression. In the expression of the times, the conservatives were "coming out of the woodwork."

13. See Beck (1986) and a response by Weisberg (1986) for intriguing analyses of the directions in which the study of voting might have developed but did not. Weisberg shows that a number of alternative issues in voting flowered before the advent of surveys of voting behavior, each more or less abandoned as the psychology of voter choice became the one ring of a one-ring circus.

2

The Concept of
Policy Mood

Since out of drift and incoherence, settled aims do appear, there must be . . . a national mind, a spirit of the age which imposes order upon random opinion.

—**Walter Lippmann**, *Public Opinion*

General Social Survey (GSS) interviewers in the field might have noticed in February 1980 that, with few exceptions, on question after question—on whether we should take measures to equalize wealth between rich and poor; on whether we were spending enough for such problems as health, the environment, and big cities; on whether police permits should be required for gun purchases; on whether the federal income tax was too high; and so forth—there were fewer liberal responses and more conservative ones than there had been in the last survey. Sometimes a lot fewer and a lot more, but in the norm a percentage point or two or three. And the same had been true the previous February: more conservatives and fewer liberals than the year before. And before that, again the same. And interviewers for Trendex, Roper, Gallup, and the National Election Study (NES)—for all the organizations that sampled public opinion with some regularity—talking to different respondents at varying times might have noticed the same pattern. And all who continued to watch might have noticed a reversal of that pattern after 1980, when there began to be more liberals and fewer conservatives year by year.

Over the errors and fluctuations inherent in the survey enterprise, interviewers talking to real people about their views might have seen a pattern. Not merely a response to guns or taxes, to cities or health care, environment, or wealth, that pattern was more general, a changing mood in the electorate. Not merely "improving and protecting the natural environment" or taxes "too high, about right, or too low," it was global, a different feeling about most of the things government did, a different feeling about government itself. Perhaps it was the sum of many different people reacting separately to many different issues, each in its own terms. But it is unlikely that the terms of each issue should have moved independently in the same direction at the same time. Perhaps it was this "mood" itself, a single factor, that changed.

Mood is a familiar notion in other aspects of life. And it finds its way into politics in the musings of commentators. But mood is not a well-defined idea in scholarly treatments of public opinion. Making some sense of it in scientific terms is the principal function of this chapter. This word itself, *mood* (which I use as shorthand for policy mood or domestic policy mood), is intended to be a scientific alias for what Lippmann called, with some skepticism, the "spirit of the age." It connotes shared feelings that move over time and circumstance. Not "moody," meaning fickle, erratic, emotional, *mood* here captures the idea of changing *general* dispositions. In everyday usage, when we are angry, depressed, cheerful, optimistic—whatever—about everything, we call it a mood. Policy mood is the same idea applied to policies and publics; it implies that publics see every public issue through general dispositions. Tied to the language of psychology, its content is political. I conclude in the end that it looks also to be consistent with assumptions about rational behavior, that is to say, well out of the customary realm of psychology.

The Dynamics of Public Policy Preference: A Model of Public Opinion

Where one presumes that public opinion is no more than the answers to opinion, belief, and preference questions in surveys, which is pretty much the norm in this highly operationalist domain, then no further substantive model is required.[1] But that approach can't yield a set of rules for how we might measure a concept. It simply tells one that the measure *is* the measure.

The familiar lore of political eras—the liberal 1960s, the Reagan revolution of the 1980s, and so forth—carries no explicit model. It is what it is without much reflection. That is why it is political lore and nothing more. But a systematic view of policy mood, as it might drive representation, requires more. It requires us to think about what public opinion is, how we come to know it, and how it works its influence. The little model I develop here is a means to give mood a role in the larger picture of democratic politics. The development is in two stages. First, I lay out policy choice and policy preference as a spatial process for a hypothetical single choice at one moment in time. I then generalize the consequences of that static formulation to policy choice and public response as joint processes over time.

The Spatial Representation

Analysts of the interplay of public preference and public policy, at least since Downs (1957), have found it convenient to imagine a policy space—sets of alternatives arrayed left to right—common both to those who formulate policies and to the mass publics who observe them. The common space locates policy with respect to preference and preference with respect to policy. It is an analytic convenience to make policy one domain (with two aspects) rather than separate worlds. Such a policy space requires a presumption that policy might be spatially represented, that it is amenable to the idea of degree (not kind). It requires also some meaningful dimension on which the degree may be represented.

Individual citizens are presumed to have ideal points, most-preferred choices from large sets of alternatives. Those ideal points aggregated to the level of a "public" form distributions of preference. Usually they are taken as given, determined by individual values and by processes of preference formation outside the dynamic of policymaking itself. This "exogeneity of preferences" assumption is one to which I will return at the conclusion of this essay. Preference distributions are commonly assumed (for simplicity) as some variation from the family of unimodal (single-humped) distributions.[2] The convenient mathematics of the normal distribution makes it a common choice.

In the process of working through the mathematics of policy preference distributions, analysts commonly assume that the distribution is symmetrical, that it has a central tendency equidistant from left and right extremes. Symmetry is assumed, not demonstrated. Working on hypothetical exercises without empirical referents, analysts adopt symmetry because there typically is no basis for any contrary assumption. Symmetry is parsimonious. And usually it doesn't matter in any case.

Anticipating the longitudinal reformulation of the preference distribution that is to come, I find it useful to make the less restrictive assumption, that in the general case preference distributions are asymmetrical, extremes are *not* equidistant from the center (although the special case of symmetry is not ruled out as a possibility).

Presume that public opinion, as seen by professionals in the business of government and politics, consists of a tripartite typology: (1) issue positions too far left for public acceptance, (2) those similarly too far right, and (3) a zone of acquiescence between them—not necessarily exactly in the middle (see Figure 2.1).

The zone of acquiescence is a range of incremental policy choices firmly within established consensus. Because that is so, no public response is to be expected from the choice of any one of them.[3] A rational public "responds" when the differences between alternative policies are substan-

FIGURE 2.1   A Conceptual Scheme for Policy Choice in a Democracy

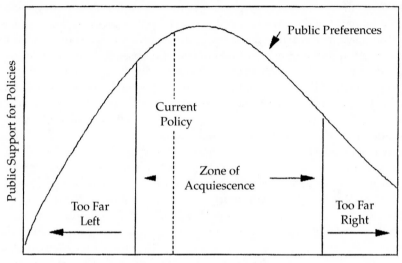

Policy Options: Liberal to Conservative

tial, when, that is, they are large enough to justify the cost of being informed and attentive. When differences are insubstantial, it is rational to be uninformed, not to notice them. The public acquiesces within the "zone," then, because the marginal cost of doing otherwise (being informed and attentive) exceeds its expected benefit.

The width of this middling zone is a function of indifference, the degree of which rests on perceived benefits of alternative courses of policy and on the costs of information on those benefits. Where real benefit differentials are modest or information costs exceed what an inattentive electorate will bear or both, then this indifferent portion of the policy space might be large. In other cases, the issue of abortion comes to mind as a good example, the policy space may reduce to unacceptable actions in either direction with no acquiescent zone.

The problem of presenting asymmetry is that it has infinite variations. Figure 2.1 illustrates one hypothetical possibility. Insofar as one can imagine left and right reversed and the degree of asymmetry varied, it is "typical." The hypothetical issue space shows current public policy to be left of center. A limited number of possibilities are still further left. But the area on the right of the status quo is larger, representing both that there are more numerous conservative choices possible (the discrete case) and that the degree of possible rightward movement is larger (the continuous case).

A rational policymaker who wished to minimax regrets (to take that course of action that would have minimum bad consequences) would stay within the zone of acquiescence. Given uncertainty about where the bounds are, one who was also cynical (i.e., willing to sacrifice his or her own, party, or government policy goals) would move to the right in this instance. I am *not* assuming that policymakers do, for the most part, behave cynically.

A real-world scenario that more or less fits the figure is the situation of Ronald Reagan at inauguration. Policy at that moment was, in general, toward the left, if not as far left as it had been, say, for the brief moment of the Great Society during the Johnson administration. And there was evidence of a public restiveness about liberal solutions, a willingness to think favorably about innovations toward the right.

The zone of acquiescence in the general case is asymmetrical; the center need not be equidistant from the bounds. That suggests that it might be the case that at any given time the electorate is more willing to tolerate policy innovation and experimentation in the one direction than the other. The zone of acquiescence notion implies a social awareness of a left-right continuum, although the process can be so passive, so driven by social communication, that most citizens might act with respect to it without being aware of it. This is not by any means "ideology" in the sense understood in the research on voting behavior. That political psychology orientation toward the structure of ideas requires far more than is needed for ideological influence to emerge as a macro phenomenon.

A Moving Zone: A Longitudinal Formulation of Policy and Preferences

If the zone of acquiescence is asymmetrical, it is a short step to the suspicion that the asymmetry might vary with time. This willingness to tolerate policy experiments more in one direction than the other flows not only from values (which might be practically fixed for a lifetime) but also from strategic premises about the effectiveness of policy approaches and the goodness and badness of particular implementations. These are driven by experience. That makes them changeable, both for individuals and publics.

If the bounds of acquiescence are allowed to move, then (turning the static representation on its side to introduce a time dimension) we can envision a moving zone that displaces up and down with context and public experience with policy experimentation. A zone of such policy consensus moving over time resembles a meandering river, a familiar metaphor of political life.

If we allow variation of asymmetry over time, then we would expect to see shifts of public preferences. If politicians sense such shifts—and everything we know about the species suggests that preference sensitivity is a finely honed attribute—then we have a basis for expecting elite behavior to conform to public mood. We expect, in other words, the acceptable center of political views to meander over time like a flowing river and for politicians to swim more or less where it goes, not to watch it from the bank.[4]

Movement over time in the value component of public preference could also produce something like the meanders of Figure 2.2. But a virtue of the notion of the zone of acquiescence is that we can imagine the bounds of acquiescence to be quite variable even when values are fixed. That produces a plausible expectation of movement over time. It requires no assumption of ideological conversion. To the degree that preferences are heavily weighted by pragmatism, a not unknown characteristic of American culture, the movement over time is all the easier and all the more likely.

Figure 2.2 presents the track through time of a hypothetical issue preference distribution, symbolized by moving bounds. The area between the bounds is constant,[5] but their displacement varies up and down. Between the bounds is the hypothetical line of real policy formation, represented as an alteration between small incremental movements and occasional jumps of some magnitude.

FIGURE 2.2   A Hypothetical Picture of Policy and Public Acquiescence over Time

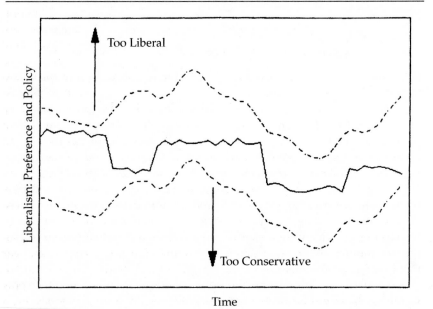

Time

How many of these meandering policy spaces ought we to expect? Is there one for each major domain of policy, one for each issue, one for each survey item, or maybe even just one? As an empirical issue, that will merit considerable attention in later analyses. But it is useful to address the hypothetical case here. Rational people engaging in information processing are cognitive misers. They do not pay the costs of complicated information-processing schemes when simple ones will serve their goals well. The usual static case for why a simple cognitive arrangement of ideas should prevail—the extraordinary cost of knowing what one needs to know to do better—is even stronger in the longitudinal realm. For the vaunted complexity of choice in the usual static scenario is about *one* choice at one time. Real individuals confront an ongoing sequence.

If there are n issues of concern to a particular citizen, the cost of information and decision processing, c becomes $n*c$ for heroic individuals who wish to treat each as separate and distinct. And those likely to be willing to bear heroic costs for political information processing are likely to be the very same set of individuals for whom n is very large. Interest in politics produces both the willingness and the n. The consequence is that $n*c$ is likely to dominate the utilities to be derived from complicated information processing across the scale of political attentiveness. Those (larger numbers) at the inattentive end of the scale need economical preference formation because the perceived utilities of politics are too small to justify more elaborate schemes. Those at the attentive end need them because they use them so much.

Here too we need to recall the social organization of belief. We read politics not as facts from a printout but as shared ideas from social and political interaction. We needn't work through the logic of what is a liberal or conservative position on policy x, when friends, neighbors, co-workers, and nightly guests who enter our living rooms through the TV set are there to tell us. And if we borrow our ideas from Teddy Kennedy or Ronald Reagan—or any number of other people who might in turn have borrowed from them—then we borrow a consistent bipolar conception of the world. Individuals grappling with the logic of complex issues might evolve a complex scheme of values and judgments. Borrowers will borrow the scheme that's there. What's there, constantly ordered by a party system offering choices between two options, is a unidimensional scheme, left to right. In politics only very few are professionally involved in issues. Most of us necessarily are on the periphery; most of us are borrowers.

The conclusion that follows this line of reasoning, if not elegantly, is that some summary dimension is likely to produce simple (hence parallel over time) response across issues for many individuals. And what emerges for many individuals separately emerges powerfully in aggregates. This implies a latent continuum underlying expressed policy preferences, a *common* cause of somewhat diverse opinions that produces observable parallelism in the movements of policy preferences over time. In other words, it implies that it is simpler to see issues in bundles than each on its own terms and that tracks of issue preferences over time should move together, tracing more or less parallel courses.

This bundling of issue preferences as if the separate issues were not really separate is policy mood. A macro-level concept, it emerges in aggregates. It is seen in electorates, not in individuals. Its roots are *both* in individual psychology and in social communication, and thus it might emerge from the latter even if (hypothetically) totally absent in the former.

Whether issue preferences move together over time is a simple enough matter to observe. That is much of the focus of this essay. As the derivation of expected parallelism is loose, we will see also cases where issue preferences don't seem to be parallel. Getting in and out of wars, for example, has little in common with the domestic policy domain. But the thesis that arises from this longitudinal perspective on issue preferences is that most policy preferences are driven by a latent global attitude set, policy mood. The causal model to be entertained is that the specifics (expressed policy preferences) are indicators of a latent concept, mood, expressing a common attitude set that drives them.

Issue Dynamics:
Trends, Cycles, Stationarity?

What are aggregate policy preferences, and what should be expected of them over time and changing circumstance? Policy is the strategic implementation of valued outcomes. Each policy debate typically engages two judgmental components, which values should be pursued (and usually at the expense of which others) and which strategies are effective means of realizing the chosen values.

Values and Value Trade-offs

Of all the influences on political debate in a nation, values are probably the closest to being constant over time. Rooted as they are in the surrounding culture and only mildly the product of political life, we would not go far from the mark assuming values to be constant.

But interesting policy debates are rarely single-valued. They become interesting precisely because they require trade-offs of alternative values, neither of which can be optimized. The whole series of conflicts over the role of government in society, for example, pits unquestioned (probably unchanging) values for public health and safety, environmental quality, and so forth against the freedom not to be constrained by regulation. We can see such conflicts as single-valued—and the public probably often does—only by a process of adversarial misunderstanding, by denying that trade-offs exist.[6] In an era of environmental enthusiasm, for example, we might regard the freedom-from-constraint end of the question as so trivially valued as not to be valued at all. But if such were truly the case, and not just a temporary misunderstanding, the issue would be easily resolved, no longer on government's plate. We would choose the valued alternative over the unvalued one, and the issue would be settled for all time, ceasing in effect to *be* an issue.

If we concede that issues usually involve value trade-offs, achieving some by compromising others, the relative constancy of values ceases to be much of an anchor for policy preference, because it is possible—even likely—that constant values can produce variable value trade-offs over time. In A vs. B, we always value both A and B. But changing circumstance might well lead rational electorates to change the A/B cut point, how much A is to be sacrificed to gain how much B.

The painful debate over abortion rights is a prime example of value trade. Except for the purpose of debate over this issue, it seems likely that most Americans do truly value something like a fetal right to life, not as an absolute and for most not as a legal standard, but something to be sacrificed to a higher value, not a thing ceteris paribus of no value whatsoever. And so do they value the woman's right to choose what will become of her own body and life, an easy extension in beliefs about the values of similar freedoms where the trade-off is not in question. This is not something to be sacrificed for nothing, only for a higher value. Both values can be constant, yet at the same time the much more difficult matter of trade-off is free to move back and forth over time.

If typical issues are value trades, there remains the possibility of single-valued conflicts. Something must weigh on the other end of the scale or the issue would not be an issue. But if that something is not a cherished value, perhaps only a fondness for things as they are, then we can imagine issues with distinctive life histories. The status quo as a value has an odd property: If the status quo A is changed to "not A," then "not A" becomes the new status quo. Thus the contest "A vs. status quo" temporarily resolved in favor of A is permanently resolved in favor of A *if the status quo is the only value on one side of the equation.* Not at all a common situation, this sort of scenario may be a good fit to two peculiar issues in American politics, the social roles of blacks and women. Both groups were disadvantaged by a status quo of customarily inferior standing when the issues arose. In both cases that inferior standing was sanctioned by widespread belief that it was the natural order of things. And in both the status quo changed, apparently permanently, in the direction of a new belief in equality of role.[7]

What we may expect of the single-valued issue is that once on the agenda of public debate, it is likely to be resolved over the long haul. For it lacks the value trade-off that gives relative permanence to most conflicts. What we do see in these cases is a trend over time toward full belief in equality. These pure value issues (but not associated conflicts over implementing values) should disappear from political discourse in the long haul and will disappear as measured preferences when the numbers preferring inequality become too small for analytic interest.

Thinking and Rethinking Strategy

Policy preferences are not only value conflicts. They are powerfully influenced by strategic thinking as well. Issues are rarely so simple as "What's good?" Commonly they involve determining "what is a good way to get to" valued outcomes—full employment, racial justice, clean air, or whatever. They are strategic. We debate what strategies are useful and economic means to achieve consensual goals.

But strategies are experiential, not a priori commitments. "What works?" is a pragmatic matter. And unlike the values that may be nearly constant for individuals and societies, judgments about effectiveness of policy approach should alter with time and experience. If policymaking is not "experimental" in the sense of research design, it clearly is so in the looser sense of tentative moves toward problem solutions subject to continuing evaluation. We try out policies, and political debate subsequently reflects upon their success. The design for evaluation lacks elegance, but what matters is that we do it. We ask questions like, "Does the improvement in health and safety in the workplace justify the cost of regulation?" In political rhetoric, the answers to such questions usually seem an immutable yes or no. But individuals and aggregates judging thus are subject to cycling, as strategies are tried out and found costly or ineffective. Preferences then are not fixed for all time but are changeable with experience and with changes in social context.

Cycle and Trend

We have in hand a working definition of *trend*. We have a similar need for the term *cycle*. By (public opinion) cycle I mean nothing more than a simple combination of two things, that public opinion moves (that it does not merely fluctuate in place around a fixed equilibrium) and that movement is followed eventually by reversal. This is a weak notion of cycling. It lacks expectation of regularity of period or regularity of amplitude. Successive cycles might be longer or shorter in time. They might be weaker or stronger in the distance they move from a starting point. And they need not necessarily return to exactly where they started. All these characteristics of regular cycles in the physical world require some exactly repeatable phenomenon as cause. That we do not expect in politics.

Weak cyclical phenomena are ubiquitous. They characterize all sorts of in-between kinds of movements that neither go off indefinitely in one direction (trend) nor always stay in place. They are not cycles at all in a mathematical sense; those require the regular or periodic causes that we have denied of public opinion.

The reversal part of movement and reversal is easy enough to see from data, not a sophisticated idea. But what about movement? How can we know that opinion really moves on some issue rather than just fluctuating? There are technical answers to this question of real movement (integration) or fluctuation in place (stationarity). I wish to stress instead some intuition about the matter.

To say that movement is real is to say roughly that some movement from level A to level B establishes an expectation that the level of the future series is changed. A stationary series perturbed from its equilibrium tends quite quickly to return to it. Genuine movement in issue series creates meander, a tendency to wander back and forth in lazy sequences, staying for years at a time in either the liberal or conservative ranges.

Determining which it is, equilibration or meander, is still hard for the unpracticed eye. For aid we look at a typical meandering series, a Trendex item on doing more for health, and ask what it would look like if it were instead stationary. The meander in a meandering series comes from the moving expectation. It may be modeled as a series S_t, a function of its own previous value S_{t-1} and the current year fluctuation a_t, which we understand to be a combination of both purely random variations (such as sampling error) and of true movements idiosyncratic to year t:

$$S_t = S_{t-1} + a_t, \qquad [2.1]$$

whereas a truly stationary series of the same movements would be

$$S_t = \bar{S} + a_t, \qquad [2.2]$$

the whole question resolving to whether the moving S_{t-1} or the constant mean best represents the expected level of the series.

Figure 2.3 illustrates the difference. It shows in the upper portion the actual proportions taking the liberal "do more" positions on the health care indicator. We can easily solve 2.1 for the disturbance term a_t and ask what it would look like if it fluctuated around a constant mean as in 2.2.

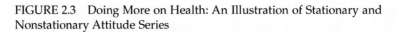

FIGURE 2.3   Doing More on Health: An Illustration of Stationary and
Nonstationary Attitude Series

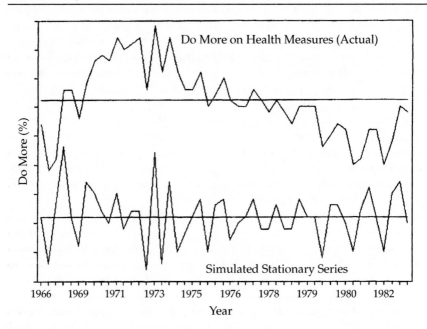

That is the lower portion of the figure. That lower portion shows the
health series as it would look if it were truly stationary. It shows all of the
real variation, that is, except the moving expectation.

With picture and intuition, now we can ask whether the movements
over time seem to be movement and reversal or just random fluctuation
around an unmoving equilibrium. It is easily seen that forcing the series
to vary around a constant mean changes its character considerably, that
the bottom of the figure is a different story from the top. The movement
is real.

Cycles as Waves

If there is a good physical analogy to the cycles of issue opinion, to
movement and reversal, it is not pendulum or orbit. Those produce perfectly repeated behaviors. The ocean wave, peaks followed by troughs
followed by peaks, is a closer fit. But some peaks are large and some are
small. And the troughs are not uniform either. The cross section is similar, one wave to another, but not uniform. If the average is, say, 50 feet
peak to peak, trough to trough, then waves of just 30 or as many as 100

feet are still waves. The concept doesn't require uniformity. But it imposes limits. A 1,000-foot cross section we would call something other than a wave. Regular cycling is associated with peaks and troughs of roughly similar size.

Cycles are ubiquitous in public views of politics. But they are not quite universal. The rare "issue" trends instead. Why it does so and why doing so is rare requires explanation. The familiar distinction between ends and means is the beginning of one explanation.

Ends and Means: Goals and Policies

Few ends are controversial, and so we rarely regard them as "issues" and rarely measure support for them in surveys. If we asked, for example, "Should every American who is willing to work for it have a right to a job and a decent standard of living?" the result would approach unanimity as a cross section and would be a time series without interesting variation. The idea isn't controversial as a goal. It's when we ask about means, what government should *do*, that controversy arises. The goals of political life are numerous. Each is a potential time series. But these are mainly time series that don't exist, because we don't find them controversial enough to be grist for survey research. The few that do exist present a selection bias. They are measured precisely because they are atypically controversial.

When goals become issues in themselves—black's and women's equality, for example—then (and only then) do we measure support for ends. We ask, for example, "Should women have an equal role?" Support for ends in these relatively rare cases probably has no equilibrium level that can be sustained under controversy. One or the other side "wins," and then attitudes move unidirectionally toward consensus. So it is not that value issues tend to trend. Most are stable and monotonous. But in the rare cases where value questions are controversial—which is when we measure them in surveys—resolution (hence trend) is to be expected.

Why are issues as means different? The issue as measured is usually a variation on "What steps should government take (and what alternative utilities should be sacrificed) to deal with unachieved values?" Implicitly, and not uncommonly explicitly, that means what steps *relative to what government is currently doing.*

Absolutes permit movement toward consensus—women should have an equal role, de jure segregation is wrong. But relatives—government should do more (less)—are self-equilibrating. If government follows social consensus, then its current set of policies is at an optimum support level. The next steps are likely always to be controversial. If we were to ask for a response to the statement, "Government should do more to ensure equal opportunity for women in every aspect of life even if it means that men's opportunities will have to be curtailed," we would not expect easy consensus, now or perhaps ever. Policies as means, policies as value trade-offs, equilibrate. We expect preferences over them to move as the values they trade off gain or lose weight, but we expect them never to be resolved. That is why they are interesting.

One can make an empirical assertion about the incidence of issues of the trending and cycling sort. The former are two or three out of a hundred, the latter everything else. This assertion is based upon the decisions of survey designers, for that, not the real political world, is where survey "items" come from. But I see no reason to expect survey design to emphasize the one or the other out of proportion to its actual levels of interest and controversy.

The trending issues are usually not included in the analyses to come.[8] Choosing to include them, when the direction of their trend is known a priori, tends to force one's results to (try to) fit the trend. Because they are so few and do not share their dynamics with the more common cycling issues, they cannot force a trend in estimates of mood. About all they can do is make well-behaved estimates harder to obtain.

Trend, stationarity, and cycle so far are descriptions of issue series. They are concepts that fit patterns, protocols of longitudinal variation. But *why* cycle or trend or nothing requires explanation. Its character will be brief and suggestive. A full-blown explanation of why public opinion might move as it does is a topic for another day.

Two Stories About Cycles

There are only three possibilities for the development of public mood over time: constancy, unidirectional movement, or cyclical movement. I develop briefly two models of the policy process that suggest, along with intuition and history, that cyclical movements are to be expected. Either is sufficient to produce the result.

Policy Excess. A first explanatory model is an overcompensating negative feedback system. Negative feedback systems, whether engineered, as in missile guidance systems, or natural, as in the auto driver staying in the lane by making little corrections every time the car moves too far one or the other way, have the common characteristic of adjusting to inputs of information about how things are going. The adjustments are negative in the sense that what is observed is error, and so correction is always in the other direction.

Assume that policymakers, both elected and unelected, get satisfaction from the implementation of preferred policies, and a subset of them, elected officials, also seeks election and reelection. The electorate benefits from and desires the implementation of a preferred set of policies. Assume also that the policy preferences of the mass electorate are not constant but move over time, and further that policymakers perceive that movement, although imperfectly. Then that subset of policymakers toward whom the movement occurs senses the possibility of enacting policies closer to its preferred position. The subset of policymakers who sees movement away from its preference senses possible frustration of its policy goals from action at an inopportune time. As a result, even though no policy actor changes preferences, the net policy result shifts in the direction of the movement of mass opinion.

Policymakers move in policy increments. They move, that is, not to their real preferences (which might be quite extreme relative to current policies and relevant to what the public will accept) but rather step-by-step in the direction of those preferences. At each time, t, $t + 1$, $t + 2$, and so on, they both enact new increments (moving steadily in the direction of mass opinion) and observe the reaction of the public to previous increments. Each observation serves to strengthen and confirm the initial perception of what the public wants. The process continues until some point $t + k$ when the policymakers sense negative reaction, at which point they correct their imperfect knowledge of public opinion and reverse course. This is negative feedback.

Assume that policy implementation produces a full public response only after several periods because policy implementation is not instant and response has a cumulative character. Response to policy change occurs only after the change has been in place long enough for the public to come in contact with it repeatedly. This is a natural result of the fact that the public is inattentive to politics and policy; not paying much attention to policymaking, it comes to be aware of change after it encounters its effects. But numerous encounters with policy change usually will take some time, often some years.

The public also has imperfect information about its own preferences. It is not adept in anticipating the costs of hypothetical policies and therefore cannot with certainty be predicted to continue to support policies once the real impacts of change are driven home. What is the basis for this assumption? Because political rhetoric is unbalanced, rational policy advocates will sell policy by presenting it as cost-free sets of benefits. They succeed often in selling policy proposals to the electorate, the *net* effect of which could not have been successfully advocated. Information about costs and other trade-offs increases after implementation, based upon real experience, leading to apparent flip-flops in public sentiment, caused more by improved understanding than by changed preferences.[9]

Thus the point at which negative public response is sensed is not when policy has gone just beyond what the public wants but rather k periods later, when policy has continued to overshoot public preference for both time and distance and is now outside the range of acquiescence. The electorate then reacts to policy excess and, in light of new information about policy effects, shifts preferences in the contrary direction, a shift that gains momentum over the k periods while the excess continues to grow before policymakers change course. When policymakers perceive the shift, the process begins anew in the opposite direction until, eventually, it too overshoots public acquiescence and causes another reversal.

The one most essential requisite for all negative feedback systems to work effectively is that the feedback be timely. If it is not, then small continuous corrections do not produce a smooth path. If corrections are late, they will be large and discontinuous. Large, discontinuous corrections produce cycling. If corrections are too large and too late, the character of the cycling becomes ever more violent and unstable.

This model fits policymaking as a short-term adaptive enterprise. The next moves to a longer-term conception and asks what must happen to a policy regime long in place.

Policy Regimes. Presume that policymaking is characterized by regimes, periods in which policy direction is mainly liberal or mainly conservative. Such regimes might be driven by mass preferences, through elections or otherwise, but they need not be. They could, for example, be the incidental result of throwing out a previous set of rascals on performance grounds. All that is important is that they occur and that they are perceived by the electorate to occur.

Regimes always are perceived to fail to perform in the long term. Even if success were possible, perception of failure is likely to cumulate over the duration of the regime. In the worst case, even if policy A works brilliantly to solve problem A, the mass electorate will ultimately reject the regime because it fails to perform on some other problem B (which might indeed only become a "problem" because success on A creates an issue vacuum that needs to be filled by new problems). One can imagine relatively long regimes or relatively brief ones, but it is hard to imagine permanence. Failures must occur, and ultimately they must be blamed on the policies in place.

The natural result must be that the longer a regime is in place, the more it will come to be associated with failure, leading to increasing probability of reversing direction. Policy regimes are thus expected to produce policy moods that cycle back and forth over the long term. The process is not so regular or determined that anything like regular periods of alteration can be expected. But it does lead to the reasonable expectation that a mature policy regime is more likely to experience reversal than indefinite continuation.

Arthur Schlesinger puts it with more color:

> Disappointment is the universal modern malady. . . . It is also a basic spring
> of political change. People can never be fulfilled for long either in the pub-
> lic or in the private sphere. We try one, then the other, and frustration com-
> pels a change in course. Moreover, however effective a particular course may
> be in meeting one set of troubles, it generally falters and fails when new
> troubles arise. And many troubles are inherently insoluble. As political eras,
> whether dominated by public purpose or by private interest, run their
> course, they infallibly generate the desire for something different. It always
> becomes after a while "time for a change." (1986:28)

NOTES

1. We would still benefit from methodological sorts of theories and models, theories of the survey response itself, see Feldman (1990), and Zaller and Feldman
(1988).

2. But see Dahl's (1956) *A Preface to Democratic Theory,* where alternative forms
and their implications are worked out.

3. By *public,* I mean here the general public, not including numerically minor
groups ("issue publics") so directly involved in process, policy, and consequences
as to be responsive to every imaginable policy choice.

4. One can imagine politicians with fixed preferences about policy who
nonetheless adjust their tactical views to the currents of the day from the belief
that changing the direction of the mainstream requires one to be in touch with it,
if not in its center. If we grant the common assumption that professional politicians harbor stronger and more ideological views than the citizens they represent,
then the ability to make such tactical adjustments, adopted consciously or otherwise, must be a well-honed skill. This is not a cynical suggestion that politicians
adopt views only for expediency—a view I cannot reconcile with firsthand experiences with elected politicians—but rather an assertion that the requisite of influence is tactical adaptation to circumstance, an important component of which
is the mood of the times.

5. This assumption too could reasonably be generalized. I do not do so because
it is beyond the available data to estimate bounds of acquiescence at all, let alone
the distance between them. It is a concept without any but arbitrary measurement
in this essay.

6. If this adversarial scenario of public understanding of issue debates is correct, it would lead to the expectation that the ignored side of the trade-off would
later give pain and cause its reassertion. If the originally valued alternative becomes similarly undervalued against the pained alternative, we have a teeter-
totter pattern of cycling back and forth over the long haul.

7. I do not wish to imply that racial or gender prejudices have disappeared and
certainly not that new beliefs in equality imply support for government efforts to

effect a change in status. These are separable issues. What can be shown to have changed is that most once believed inequality itself was right and no longer do.

8. Happily, that decision need not be arbitrary or a priori. Leaving them in the issue matrix for the recursive maximum likelihood estimator, to be developed in Chapter 3, tends to produce communality estimates that converge on zero, giving trending issues no weight in final estimates, whether or not included.

9. The process could be ameliorated by analytic treatment of policy proposals in public media, but that tends to be blunted by the conflict between analysis and entertainment, which is the central consideration for commercial media, particularly television. Analysis makes us informed about choices but isn't entertaining. A profit-driven system of public information, propelled by consideration of circulation or ratings, will therefore systematically fail the needs of democracy.

3

Developing a
Measure of Mood

Domestic policy mood is the concept. It arises from a view of public opinion as an aggregate entity. We expect it to cycle back and forth, left and right, as leaders and followers change their views of government policy over time, sometimes believing that particular policies work and sometimes that they don't, sometimes open to that next experiment in the public order and sometimes not.

But we haven't seen this thing, mood. We don't yet know if there even is an "it" that can be said to exist. Or if it is really "them," all kinds of little moods running hither and yon, global only in limited domains. Concepts are cheap. What we really want is a concept and a set of empirical operations that exemplify it. What we want is a measure, and that is what this chapter is about. We ask what the problems are with measuring mood; we find out they are many. And we develop many schemes to cope with those many problems. And we decide on one best scheme. We begin with a look at the raw materials from which a measure is to be extracted.

The Survey Marginals Data Base

The starting point of mood is information on specific preferences. Not quite "raw" data, survey marginals are the descriptive result of individual surveys, the percentage choosing the various possible responses to survey items. The case is each item each time it is administered. The desired final measure is a regular time series, regular in the sense of having exactly one value for each period, normally a year. Such discipline, alas, must be imposed. The data don't come in such a convenient form. Survey researchers ask questions when they feel like asking them, and rarely does that feeling come at regular intervals.

Survey items may be conceptualized as time series. All the administrations of a particular item, that is, form a series, ordered by time. The first and most basic selection criterion for items, then, is that they must be repeated; the one-shot item gives no leverage on change. Spacing in the time dimension is not, in general, uniform. And that is true within as well as between particular items. Not chaotic (in the old, loose sense of that word), for time itself is perfectly orderly, the spacing is disorderly with respect to intervals. "Adjacent" administrations of an item may be separated by ten days or ten years. Within a series, one item might even have both. At the level of the data base, then, the survey results—the marginal percentages for and against—are ordered by time (in years, months, and days, dated by the first day of fieldwork). No two items, in general, have the same number of administrations. Nor, in general, are administrations at the same times across items. There is, in short, no parallel structure in the data base. It is a bunch of items ordered internally by date but externally (between items) by nothing. Aggregation into regular time periods is imposed by the analyst, not a natural property of the items themselves.

The structuring element that distinguishes this collection from looser alternatives, such as that maintained by the Roper Center archive, is that the various administrations are maintained as series of the same question over time. (Roper, in contrast, treats each administration as an isolated unit of information, not linked to past or future.) The creation of series of "the same" item administered at various times requires some researcher discretion about what is or is not the same. One may be rigid or relaxed in such judgments. I err on the side of rigidity, in part from unhappy experience with the alternative. Absolute rigidity, however, wastes information. Some wording differences are plainly minor. If a question sometimes asks whether "the national government" and sometimes "the government in Washington" should do something, it doesn't make a discernible difference in the response, or so at least it seems. Wording differences on that scale are tolerated.

Any kind of filter mechanism, on the other hand, even the innocent-sounding, "or haven't you thought very much about that?" tagged onto an otherwise identical question, produces substantially different marginals.[1] Filtered and unfiltered versions of "an" item therefore must be treated as wholly independent items, with the regrettable loss of information that entails. Artifactual "changes" in policy preference are much the greater evil than information loss.

A relational data base, the information is structured on two levels: by item description, all those attributes such as the question text and response options that are fixed over time, and by responses, the numeric information that varies with administration. The data may then be characterized by the number of items (145) and the number of administrations (2,056) of them.

Information about survey marginals is reported in various places: newspapers (and news releases); periodic reports, such as those produced by the Gallup Poll; codebooks for academic surveys; secondary analyses in scholarly journals; data compendia; and archives. Most often they are reports of one administration of an item. Occasionally, whole series are published, for example, the particularly useful compendium of Niemi, Mueller, and Smith (1989) or the lengthy series of scholarly analyses of Shapiro and various co-authors in "The Polls" section of *Public Opinion Quarterly* (1984a, 1984b, 1985, 1986, 1987). The Roper Center POLL on-line access service is of unique value for a data collection of this sort. Its coverage of topics and survey houses (both commercial and academic) is quite broad. Almost a single source for public opinion marginals, it has two limitations that required broader search for this study: It doesn't include National Election Study materials (or even all of the Roper Center holdings), and its coverage of all materials thins as one goes back in time, particularly before the early 1960s. Collecting one series from more than one source must be done with considerable care, because there are (in addition to comparability problems in the items themselves) incomparabilities in reporting survey marginals. Survey research lacks a protocol for reporting findings. And a difference as small as inconsistent reports of percentages—arising from whether or not the "not ascertained, not available, not asked" response categories are included in the totals from which percentages are calculated—will distort an item series.[2]

The direction of a particular response, liberal or conservative, must be assigned. For domestic issues, that is both easily done and robust.[3] One can debate for hours about the inherent meaning, if any, of the concepts of liberal and conservative. But the judgment of direction of survey responses is typically quite simple.[4] And because mistakes would have produced evidence of error—the miscoded series would move contrary to others to which it should be similar—the judgments are robust. If issue time paths were independent of one another, coding direction might produce a quandary or two. When they are parallel, as we will see they are, every series serves to validate every other. Information about degree or intensity of response is included in the data base but not exploited in any of the measures to be developed.

The criteria for inclusion of survey marginals are (1) that they be issue preferences, sometimes interpreted loosely, and (2) that they be measured in identical form in more than one year. Many thousands of survey results meet the first criterion. A smaller, but still substantial, number also meet the second. The great majority of them concern domestic policy preferences, both because there are more domestic than foreign policy materials to start with and because the domestic arena is the main stage of policy mood.

Building to a measure, upward from a set of items, produces a result that clearly depends upon what items were initially selected for analysis. To have confidence in the measure, we need to have confidence that the selection process was broadly representative of available materials. One means to attain that goal is to minimize researcher discretion in selection, to take everything that can be found. Within the domestic policy sphere that is how I proceed.[5]

Analyses below use all items, with no researcher discretion (beyond the collection stage) involved. But some of the items drop out at the measurement stage, where, lacking common association with other items, their weight goes to zero, or effectively so. This is true in particular of foreign policy (not including defense) items and of two racial and gender equality preferences, which trend toward uniform acceptance of equality.

But the "what" of the data bases can best be seen with examples. The measurement problem is laid out here in stages, beginning with some examples that present no problems and then moving on to the typical—and typically problematic set.

Example Analysis 1:
GSS Domestic Spending Priorities

It is useful at the outset to develop some intuition on the measurement of policy mood. The raw series are a good beginning point. Figure 3.1a displays six questions about domestic spending priorities posed in the General Social Survey in common format since 1973, (except in 1979, 1981, 1992, and 1995, when the GSS was not fielded). Each begins with the lead, "We are faced with many problems in this country, none of which can be solved easily or inexpensively. I'm going to name some of these problems, and for each one I'd like you to tell me whether you think we're spending too much money on it, too little money, or about the right amount." The survey then references a specific area where respondents are asked: "Are we spending too much, too little, or about the right amount on" the area in question (cities, health, education, environment, conditions of blacks, and welfare). The common format and frame of reference produce unusually well-behaved time series, free from many of the problems that more typically make it difficult to see association between policy preferences. The series are graphed here as a liberalism index, which is simply the percentage of liberal responses (pro-spending on these items) divided by the percentage of liberal and conservative responses. Thus, for example, in 1973 on the question of welfare, 20 percent said "too little" and 51 percent "too much," resulting in an index value of $20/(20 + 51) = 28.2$. These well-behaved items allow a clean look at the business of cross-series association over time.

FIGURE 3.1a   Liberalism for Six GSS Spending Series: Raw Liberalism Index

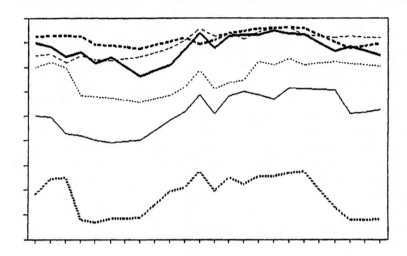

A quick look at the figure might suggest that the six are only loosely connected. But that is an illusion of the graphic presentation. The eye sees the substantial over-time differences between series: Education spending is popular and welfare is not (which is irrelevant to the question of movement over time). But the eye fails to see how closely the series move in parallel. The series in fact are highly correlated, as can be seen in Table 3.1, with only three of the fifteen between-series correlations less than .5 and the highest at .88.[6]

TABLE 3.1   Correlations Between GSS Spending Items

	Cities	Education	Environment	Welfare	Health
Cities					
Education	0.51				
Environment	0.65	0.73			
Welfare	0.50	0.50	0.71		
Health	0.48	0.41	0.73	0.75	
Race	0.68	0.88	0.81	0.65	0.59

Note: N = 20

One way to "see" the true association is to remove the differences in the average level between series. The effect of those substantial differences is to stretch the vertical range and, by doing so, flatten the series traces. Figure 3.1b undoes that by forcing all the series to have a mean level the same as the original average of all six. The modest parallelism of the earlier figure is considerably less modest when the series are forced to vary in the same range. It is immediately apparent that they have something in common, a movement toward high levels of conservatism around 1980 that dissipates thereafter.

Some series vary more than others, and that too tends to hide some of the true association over time. Figure 3.1c uncovers a bit more of the common movement by also forcing series variation to be the same across the six. Because the variances are similar (in this case) to start with, standardizing them has much less visual impact than did setting the series to the same means.

All that remains to uncover a "domestic spending priorities mood" is to discard the particulars of each issue, the squiggles in a particular year that each series does not share with the others. Figure 3.1d does that, presenting the average of the six fully standardized series as an estimate of

FIGURE 3.1b   Liberalism for Six GSS Spending Series: Series Adjusted to a Common Mean

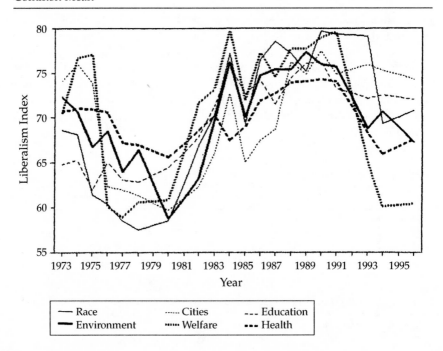

FIGURE 3.1c   Liberalism for Six GSS Spending Series: Mean and Variance
Standardized

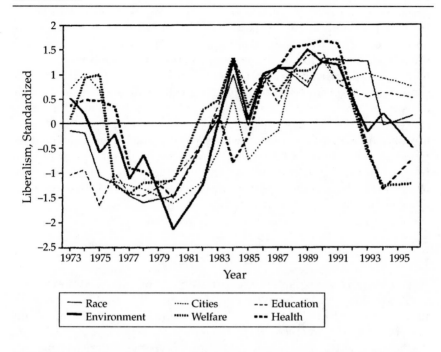

FIGURE 3.1d   Liberalism for Six GSS Spending Series: Combined, with Plus
and Minus One Standard Deviation Bounds

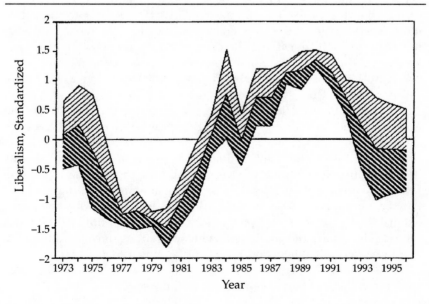

mood. To reinforce the notion of mood as a moving stream of preferences, the estimates are presented with a band of plus or minus one standard deviation (computed for each year from the six series) around them.

There is an important substantive lesson in this little illustration. It is clear that much of the variation in these spending priorities is shared with the others. If one were to tell the story of "trends in support for" each of them, it would be quite misleading to begin with an assumption that, for example, support for education spending is driven by events and conditions *in education*. It plainly is difficult to locate in any one of these six areas movement that looks like it could not be chance fluctuation around a common norm. Some there must be. But it would be small in contrast to the common shifts of underlying sentiment. That is the point of view to be taken throughout this essay, that the common movements underlying policy preference changes are considerably more "real" than the measured policy preferences themselves.

Example Analysis 2:
Trendex on Doing More

A set of items measured (almost) quarterly by Trendex (a one-time division of General Electric) is a useful second illustration. The Trendex set is a regular and well-behaved time series, like the GSS spending items, but it covers a different period (1968–1982), is measured at more frequent intervals, and focuses on the more general question of what government "does" as opposed to what it spends. All items begin with the lead: "I would like to get your opinion on several areas of important government activities. As I read each one, please tell me if you would like to see the government do more, less or do about the same amount as they have been on," and adds the issue focus in question: "helping minority groups," "education," "health measures," "expanding employment," and "urban renewal."

A simple plot of the raw series (again as a liberalism index) presents, as before, little visual evidence of association. And one could easily take a hard look at Figure 3.2a and conclude that no systematic behavior over time is in evidence. The series squiggle up and down across readings, track different average levels, and look more or less random.

As in the figures for the GSS items, the raw plot hides a good deal. Following the same strategy, except combining the standardization of level and variance in one step, the same data are presented, standardized into a common plot range, in Figure 3.2b. As before, it is quickly apparent that the figure uncovers systematic movement over time. The Trendex series (individually and combined) evidence a strong movement from liberal to conservative views on issues of the government's role from the 1970s to around 1980, which then abates and moves back in the liberal direction for the brief period until the end of the series.

FIGURE 3.2a   Five Trendex Series: Liberalism Index

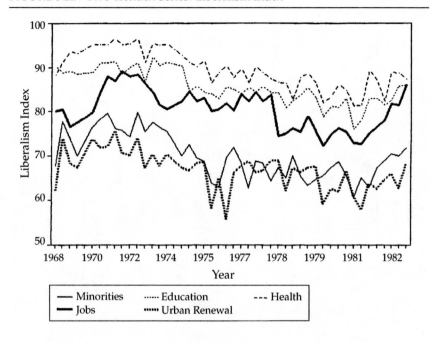

FIGURE 3.2b   Five Trendex Series: Mean and Variance Standardized

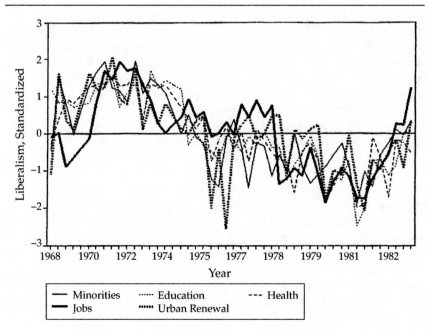

FIGURE 3.2c   Five Trendex Series: Combined, with Plus and Minus One
Standard Deviation Bounds

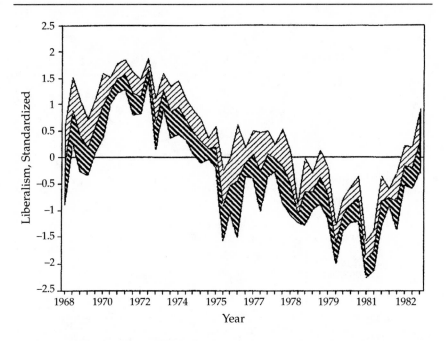

Again we proceed to abstract the central tendency of the five series
(and its variability), treating the individual measures as noisy indicators
of an underlying signal, domestic mood, or something of that character
(see Figure 3.2c). Figure 3.2c is strongly patterned over the broad sweep
of time. But its shorter-term variation, from one quarter to the next, suggests random rather than determined variation at fine time intervals. But
closure on that issue would be premature here.

We end the illustrations with a tease and a measurement conundrum.
The tease is a first, very simple look at the issue of whether these separately measured indicators show separate or similar things. To recap, we
have different survey houses asking different questions (GSS on spending, Trendex on government involvement), different time intervals (annual vs. quarterly), and different time periods (1973–1996 vs. 1968–1982).
But if something like domestic policy mood exists, they ought to track
one another to some degree, despite all the differences. That possibility is
illustrated in Figure 3.3, where they are presented together (both now annual series).

The two series do now "seem" to move together. With only eight data
points in common (recall that 1979 and 1981 readings are unavailable in

FIGURE 3.3   GSS and Trendex Combined, 1968–1996

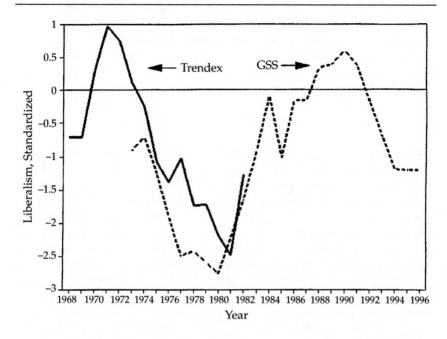

the GSS series), this is not the sort of evidence upon which one would wish to rest a test of the mood thesis. But it will do as a first illustration that something in common might be there to be found.

If these eleven items were typical of measured policy preferences for the post–World War II era, this would be a short essay. Finding their central tendencies is easy, and it is a fairly obvious idea that one should look for them. But these series were grand illustrative materials because they are so atypically good. The problem of finding the underlying movement in mood is more difficult, a lot more difficult, than simply adding up and dividing by the number of items.

The Conundrum

If this is as good as it gets, then how can we isolate an underlying mood? For that we need a longer period of time and a much broader range of issues to explore the notion in full. The intuition of the illustrative analyses will do fine, but the procedure works only so long as we have parallel items measured at all the same points in time. That we cannot have. What is known about public opinion in the post–World War II era is known from the existing record of survey marginals. It can't be redone. We have for analysis what exists. And what exists is often a mess.

Survey marginals—the simple percentage totals of those who in a given survey said yes or no, who agreed, disagreed, or whatever—are unloved by political scientists. Most particularly, they are disdained by those engaged in the survey enterprise itself. There are several reasons for this. Some will bear on the analyses to come; some will not.

The Problems: Cross-Sectional

The marginal total, first, is all but uninterpretable in isolation. If 60 percent said yes to the question and 40 percent no, what are we to make of that? Is that a lot of yesses or not? Taking one cross section at a time, we can't know. We lack a baseline with which to compare that parameter. The question itself—the particular words, that is—and its response categories can't do the job. Although the marginal is not utterly meaningless, we are left nonetheless with little more than a hunch for prior expectation of results.

Item marginals are notoriously sensitive to question wording (see Page and Shapiro [1989, 2:4–5] and Schuman and Presser [1981]). Two questions that might seem to the analyst to call for exactly the same sets of responses can prime differing respondent inclinations and attitudes, producing sometimes remarkably different marginals. Or two questions with essentially the same cues but that do or don't force respondents to choose between alternatives can have the same effect (Sullivan, Piereson, and Marcus 1978).

Even without the problems of interpretation, survey analysts would still ignore marginals most of the time because they fail to provide answers to the sorts of questions survey analysts pursue. The analysts want to know why some kinds of respondents say yes and others no, to explain attitudes in terms of the characteristics of those who hold them. The marginal totals are mute on why individuals believe what they do. As the survey researcher might put it, "Why look at a datum when data are available?"

All of these issues vanish in the context of studying opinion change over time. As part of a series ordered in time, the simple "60 percent said yes" is a datum. If it is higher or lower than readings before and after or even if it is the same, it says something about the time in which the survey was taken. And the wording of the question is controlled when it is held constant, just as it is in the cross section where the analyst compares different responses to the *same* question.[7] And one of the marginal's vices, that it ignores information about who gave which response, becomes a virtue when one wishes to examine system-level movements over time. In that case the individual responses are unwanted noise, washed out of the aggregate marginals. Those lost degrees of freedom don't look like much of a loss when, as in this essay, the numbers of individual marginals exceed the size of a typical survey sample.

The Problems: Time-Serial

But as one set of concerns vanishes, new ones arise. For survey marginals have some strange and undesirable properties as time series. They are necessarily a sample from a large number of issues that might have been probed, an infinite number of questions that might have been asked. That sample is purposive, not random. Commercial firms that sell their results as news pursue hot copy. Academic work too is haunted by the desire for immediate relevance. Before the better traditions of the 1970s, 80s, and 90s, it is clearly the case that the issue agenda of academic surveys is the agenda of the news, *current* politics.[8]

Purposive selection undermines representativeness of item selection over time. Where survey researchers measure what is current, obviously we get a set of measures heavily weighted toward the current agenda of American politics. And so we have measures of tolerance for domestic communism in the early 1950, but not after. And though support for an invigorated liberal agenda was building in the latter half of the 1950s (the buildup that ultimately flowered in the Great Society programs), it is largely unmeasured because the focus of the times was the cold war.

The implications of purposive selection are stark. If we measure issues mainly when they are hot, quite probably we measure them when attitudes are atypical. The Communist witch-hunt of the early 1950s is a good example. What little we know about attitudes toward domestic Communists and toward repressive measures against them comes from the period when these issues were briefly the central focus of American political life. When Joe McCarthy captured the attention of radio, TV, and newspapers, stirring a hornet's nest of controversy, he surely affected the attitudes we measured. And when it was over and the issue returned to the equilibrium of inattention—when we probably could have got a better fix on long-term attitudes—we stopped measuring the issues. Although this is an extreme case, it does point clearly to the error attendant upon a simple assumption that attitudes are fairly constant before, during, and after the times they are measured. The reverse is more plausible: It is likely that attitudes change between the time we measure them and the time an issue has settled down. This problem of "missing cases" presents the most difficulties in untangling the message from historical survey marginals.

It arises in more moderate form in decades'-long inattention to common issues, such as the New Deal cluster. Although we have less a priori reason to worry that attitudes were different when they weren't talked about or measured than when they were, it is nonetheless troubling to see a time series of attitudes go "underground" for a lengthy period. For balance, it should be noted that in actual numbers of missing cases, probably the majority are nearly harmless, involving, for example, alternate years that are missing in the election studies but not in other sources.

Even if we did not need to fear that missing cases might be systematically different from present ones, the simple discontinuity of the marginals series precludes use of the well-developed measurement technology of principal components and related models. Although there are means to address missing-values problems, they do not contemplate cases as bad as this one, where the modal case is missing. Here we have forty-five-year times series where perhaps ten or twelve cases are *not* missing.[9] Because these missing-value estimation techniques do not work for this case, we need to start pretty much from scratch in building a measurement technology. But before we do so, we take a look at the data not yet subject to it.

Because we are rightly suspicious of unknown, unproven analytic tools, it is useful to see the data as they are, not yet molded by assumption or technique. We can't quite do that, as we have seen with simple examples, for the human eye (and brain) can't unravel the complexity of many series that move together but are offset from one another. In order to see real longitudinal patterns of attitude change, we need to see movement on a common scale. That is problematic at the outset because it requires that we assume that available data are a representative sample from which we can estimate a mean for the series. That assumption is indefensible, which is the origin of the more complicated measurement model to come. But indefensible or not, it allows visual examination of the data before they have been processed.

A Crude Look at Problems and Prospects

Imagine for the sake of argument that what marginals really measure is latent liberal or conservative views, not attitudes toward gun control, government spending for the military, or whatever. If that is the case, we have a strange sort of time series in any array of marginals. What is strange, of course, is that except for repeated use of the same survey items, the stimuli that produce these latent views are not the same.

Just as in the cross-sectional case, where we expect items tapping the same concepts to produce similar but not identical responses, here we expect similar movement over time but not identical levels of response. This is nothing more than saying that some questions are hard to "agree" to and others are easy. And though we guess at those levels of hard and easy from the words of the questions, there is no scientific theory that tells us what words should produce what response. If any repeated application of the same questions and sampling procedures is considered a time series, then the level of the series is determined by (1) the variance it shares with policy mood, (2) an unknown but constant effect of the wording of the question, and (3) all other, uncontrolled error. Because the first component is what we wish to measure and the third is uncontrollable, the measurement problem reduces itself to finding a way to estimate and then control the question-specific effect.

Estimating the question-specific effect is easily accomplished if we can make an assumption about the observed series: that for each question, the years in which it is observed (i.e., actually posed in a survey) are typical of the whole time period under consideration. That is a very strong assumption, shortly to be abandoned as untenable. But for this "crude look" at the data it has one advantage: It permits visual examination of survey marginals as (almost) raw data, before they have been rendered into ordered time series by measurement technology that is difficult to see through.[10]

As would be expected from the preceding illustrations, the actual raw numbers in a form such as the liberalism index do not produce visual evidence of systematic movement over time in their native metrics. Such a plot would look very much like a random scatter of dots, its one systematic pattern the much greater density of readings in the 1970s and 1980s than before. What is required, as before, is a common metric that can focus attention on similarities of movement through time.

Our illustration involves all[11] domestic policy items asked more than once, 1956 to 1996.[12] If it can be assumed that the available item marginals are a representative sample of a hypothetical complete set for all years, then the means and standard deviations from the sample time series would be unbiased estimates of the full series. That (if it can be granted) justifies the arithmetic of standardization. The arithmetic still works if the assumption is wrong, but the individual series would be left miscalibrated to one another through bad estimates of their true means. Given that the point is only a picture, we can tolerate some miscalibration, a conservative error.

The point of standardization is to make the measure invariant with respect to question wording and issue domain. With it the measures of various domestic policies may be treated as a series of 2,056 points arrayed only in time. Then we can see whether there is systematic movement to be seen in survey marginals. Figure 3.4 arrays the whole "series" as dots on a standard scale. As an interpretive guide, a moving average line is plotted through the points. What can be seen in Figure 3.4 is a pattern of liberalism building in the late 1950s, briefly reversed in the late 1960s, peaking in the middle 1970s, followed by a movement to a conservative peak around

FIGURE 3.4   Domestic Policy Liberalism: Standardized Measures of All
Domestic Policy Survey Marginals

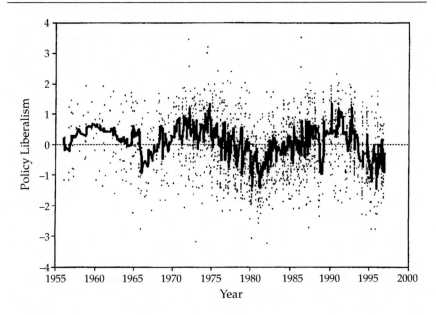

1980, and a subsequent return to liberalism. Of these, a skeptical observer
might dismiss most as fluke or insignificant shift. The distinctive V pattern
around 1980 would nonetheless require a considerable skepticism. It is not
important whether these movements are significant. They will reappear
later in similar form and with better assumptions. The important message
of the figure is that movements can be seen in the raw data.

But perhaps the pattern of Figure 3.4 is driven by a subset of measures
imposing order on what would otherwise be noise. If that were the case,
we would look for an explanation of that subset in its own issue domain—education, defense spending, the environment, or whatever—
rather than in an underlying mood. If, on the other hand, mood is driving
response to individual items, then we should see similar patterns across
domains.

Figure 3.5 breaks out a particular subset of intrinsic interest, placement
on scales of liberal or conservative self-identification. The numerous data
points associated with self-identification both permit disaggregated
analysis (on a shortened time scale) and are weighty enough to be a possible explanation of the pattern in the fully aggregated set, a threat to inference. While they remain, that is, we might mistake a pattern in the
whole for one produced by just this one set of measures.

FIGURE 3.5 Self-Identified Liberalism and Conservatism Measures on a Standard Scale

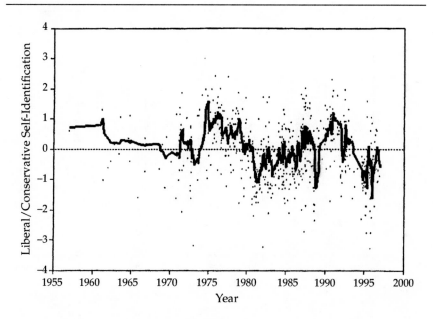

The patterns to be seen in self-identification are only partly common with the pattern of Figure 3.4. The dramatic movement toward conservatism across much of the 1970s appears in common, as does a rebounding liberalism during the Reagan years. But the rebound, if it can be called that, is tentative and limited in self-identification, not the full-scale reversal of the whole set.

Figure 3.6 shows the standardized domestic issues, as in Figure 3.4, but this time with the self-identification measures removed. If the numerous self-identification measures had provided all or part of the structure found earlier, that structure should disappear in the figure. The reverse is the case. Deprived of the self-identification measure, the remaining items of Figure 3.6 are every bit as patterned as they were with it; perhaps more so. Liberal and Conservative identification measures do not contribute to the systematic movement of mood and may, because they track a somewhat different dynamic, detract from it.

Figure 3.7 removes yet another subset, this time attitudes toward military spending. Sometimes seen as part of a foreign policy domain, sometimes as just the opposite of willingness to spend on domestic concerns, this issue domain may not belong to the whole. As before, the defense-spending domain might be suspect either because it alone contributes to

FIGURE 3.6 Domestic Policy Preference Marginals on a Standard Scale

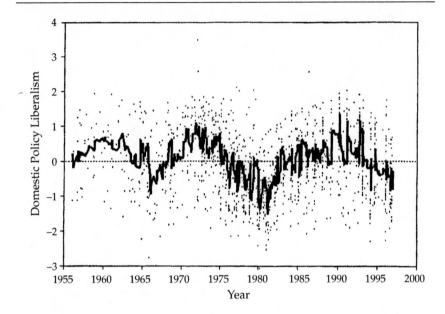

FIGURE 3.7 Domestic Policy Preference Marginals: Military Spending Items Deleted

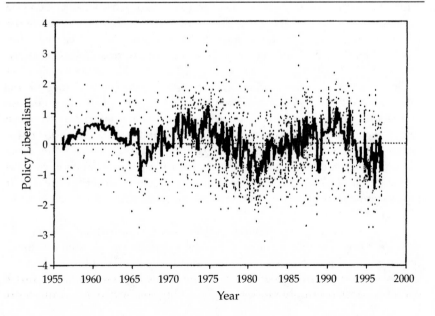

FIGURE 3.8   Preferences on Military Spending

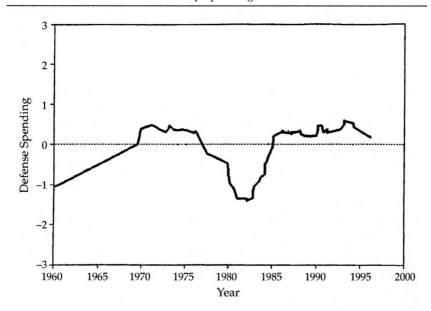

the pattern or because it violates it and doesn't belong in the set. The answer clearly is that removing the set is inconsequential. Figure 3.6 (with) and Figure 3.7 (without) are indistinguishable. Put otherwise, to know the movement of preferences on domestic issues (including spending) is also to know what to expect of the leading alternative.

The military spending measures themselves appear in Figure 3.8. Infrequently posed before the later years of the Vietnam War, the spending measures trace a dramatic liberal (i.e., against more spending) to conservative to liberal track for the twenty years beginning with 1969. This is a sharper version of the now familiar V pattern around 1980. It suggests that attitudes in this domain moved more crisply than elsewhere, but that sharp pattern could also be accounted for by the smallish set of measures.

There are dozens of ways to proceed in this vein, comparing issues, particular question formats, survey houses, and so forth. All give a similar picture. But the picture can be sharpened further.

A Regression Model for
Measuring Mood

The raw analysis we have just seen begins to reveal patterns. But it confronts a problem it cannot resolve. The problem is that the format of survey questions has changed over time. (More accurately, the proportions of questions using various possible formats has changed.) And this will systematically influence the phenomenon at hand. For format influences marginals, and that influence is not subtle.

The problem in particular is that before about the middle 1960s most policy preference questions are variations on the Likert form ("The government should do more about x"), where respondents are asked for yes or no, agree or disagree, and so forth. This style of survey item inflates the appearance of liberalism in the marginals. Its defect is that it does not ask respondents to think about the *costs* of "doing more," diverting effort from other worthy programs, budget deficits, or tax increases. Although social theorists might naively believe that anyone would understand the implicit costs and take them into account, the evidence is plainly otherwise.[13] People like programs more when they are not asked to balance benefits against costs. And from the respondent's point of view that should not be so surprising. For the respondent, after all, is not someone engaged in the business of thinking about familiar problems and solutions but is the target of unfamiliar questions from a "polite stranger" in his or her living room—and is being diverted from doing something else.[14]

The probable impact of change in format is to inflate the liberalism of the older period relative to the newer one. If we could quantify the tendency of the item to produce relatively liberal or conservative responses, that tendency could be controlled. And that suggests a solution in the form of a model of both the contribution of the particular item and the time when it was posed. If we think of a particular marginal result, M_{it}, the liberalism index for a particular item i, administered at time t, then we might explain that result as jointly the effect of the item bias, β_i, and the time, τ_t, of administration.[15] The model is 3.1:

$$M_{it} = \beta_i + \tau_t + e_{it} \qquad [3.1]$$

where e is error due neither to the item nor the time. Because we have multiple items at the same time and multiple times for each item, these effects should be separable. To separate them, however, requires us to assume again that the marginals that are available for a particular item are representative of the hypothetical set of that item measured at every time period. Otherwise the bias that we estimate will be too high or too low, and then the estimate of the time effect will also be biased. The β_i coefficient in 3.1 is of no particular interest, but its effect must be specified correctly for estimates of τ, a series of which becomes an estimate of policy mood.[16]

The regression approach takes us a step beyond calculation of means from standardized series. The regression estimates of the latent mood concept are much the same as means except that they are conditional on what survey questions happen to be available for a particular year. That should clarify the relationship of old and new formats as well as producing a smoother year-to-year pattern not so subject to the accidental variation from the on-and-off availability of series.

The regression model includes an implicit assumption that all items contribute equally to mood, that all are equally valid indicators of the concept. That assumption is certainly false (although its falsity does not seem particularly harmful). And it puts a lot of weight on the analyst's subjective judgments of what belongs and what doesn't.[17]

The virtue of this regression approach is its underlying mathematics. The general linear model is developed in an immense scientific literature. Its properties are very well known. This will be useful for validating the measurement model to come. But least squares estimation is developed for estimating structural coefficients, testing a priori specifications. The task at hand is measurement, finding numeric estimates to tap a concept. Prone to dangerous (but unlikely) errors from missing-values assumptions and unable as a practical matter to assign weights to indicators in proportion to their contributions, its role in this research program is as backstop. It will serve to demonstrate, as does the earlier presentation of simple averages, that the measurement algorithm to be developed for this problem produces estimates generally similar to those of better-known technology.

We estimate the regression model in two steps, first including only item dummy variables and then adding the time dummies as well. The first step (see Table 3.2) tells us what we fully expected to see: For all domes-

TABLE 3.2   Goodness of Fit for Regression Estimation of Mood

	Model Specification		
	Items Only $M_{it} = \beta_i + e$	Items and Time $M_{it} = \beta_i + T_t + e$	Time Only (standardized) $M_{it} = T_t + e$
R^2	.930	.948	
R^2 (adjusted)	.921	.938	.237
R^2 change		.018	.207
F (for equation)	98.83	96.40	7.93
Df (num, denom)	(120,893)	(161,852)	(40,1024)
F for change		6.89	
Df (num, denom)		(40,852)	
p for change		< .001	

Note: The liberalism index for issue i and time t is dependent in all analyses. F statistics for the second analysis are tests for the change produced by the addition of time variables.

tic policy items, 1956 to 1996, most of the variance (R^2 = .930) associated with survey marginals is associated simply with which questions are asked. This is of no importance except that it establishes an explanatory benchmark for time effects. In the second step we ask whether the time dummies might explain some of that 7.0 percent of the variance that remains after the question effects are removed. The answer is that they can. The increase in explanatory power (to R^2 = .948) is highly significant.

With 160 dummy variables in the model, one expects a good fit. The τ estimates in Figure 3.9—labeled unstandardized—are in some sense impressive. For decade-length spans they closely track the raw data, and they track alternative estimation techniques as well. Had I not lived through the 1950s, though, I'd be more impressed. The technique has the serious disadvantage of telling us that the time of Eisenhower was the pinnacle of American liberalism! That violates prior expectations, to say the least. Either something is screwy about the estimation method or our beliefs about political eras are terribly out of whack. The method is indicted.

The logic of this estimator is not the problem. The problem is that portions of the data are not rich enough to meet its needs. It can disentangle

FIGURE 3.9   Dummy Variable Regressions as Estimates of Mood for Domestic Policy

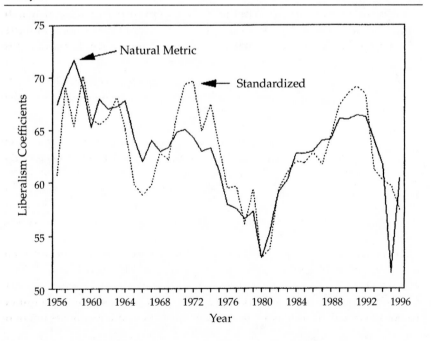

question effects from time effects so long as it has ample combinations of each. That is generally the case post 1964, where it is well behaved. Before 1964, however, there is strong collinearity of format—virtually all items are of the old Likert type—with time.[18] There is enough information to estimate coefficients, but there is not enough for the pre–1964 period to reliably disentangle time and format. The resulting compromise gives some credit for the early-period liberalism to the items and some to the times. A richer overlap of format and time would, we believe, give all the credit to the formats.

A solution suggests itself within the same logic. Because the problem is that some items produce more liberal marginals than they should, and they are typical of a particular era, standardizing *within* item series forces each series to be neutral in total contribution.[19] The method is to compute the means and standard deviations for all the available readings of each item and then compute:

$$z_t = (M_{it} - \mu_i)/\sigma_i, \qquad [3.2]$$

where μ_i is the mean of item i and σ_i is its standard deviation. (The data are also transformed for graphic convenience to produce a standardized metric similar to the original index.) After standardization, all the variation is within items and therefore within formats.

In the standardized estimation all question effects are removed by the transformation, leaving no need to model them in the regression. The fit for a standardized model falls off dramatically with all of the spurious "explanation" provided by question effects removed. But here model fit has a substantive message, that about 24 percent (or 21 percent if we adjust for the capitalization on chance inherent in fitting forty variables) of the real variance in survey marginals is associated with the time when questions are asked.

The "standardized" (dashed) series now tracks a more familiar and more plausible cycle, the pattern we have seen before with a little more precision. Without important changes in the latter part of the period, the standardization eliminates some of the artifactual liberalism of the 1950s. Very closely associated with the yet-to-be-developed recursive estimation technique, the regression procedure would be a good solution were it not that it depends upon an assumption about missing values known to be false.

The virtue of standardization is that it forces measures to discriminate *within* series over time rather than between series. One way in which the estimator is well behaved is that it is consistent with the raw data. If year t is more liberal than year u on average, based upon the items common to both years, then that same inequality appears in the estimates of latent mood. Keeping that virtue, but without having to make untenable assumptions about representativeness of available data, is the motive for a last estimation solution.

An Algorithm for Estimating Mood

Simplicity is valuable. Everything else equal, a simple measure is to be preferred to a complex one. The very simplest way to summarize a group of time series is to take their average by year. This we cannot do. For it involves adding up and dividing things like the percentages who agreed and disagreed that government "should do more to help minority groups" or "should spend more to protect the natural environment" or that "citizens should be required to obtain a police permit before they can purchase a handgun." The percentages don't mean the same thing for each. That would not be troublesome if (as in the previous illustrations) we had at least the same items every year. But we do not.

But the simplicity of the average remains attractive. We know what it means. And we know *that* it reflects its components and *how* it does so. The way to salvage this simple arithmetic is to find what comparability does exist. As a starting point, it is reasonable to assume that a survey item is comparable to its own past and future administrations.[20] If a way could be found to express each administration of an item as a ratio to some fixed reference point, for example, a particular year, then these ratios begin to look like numbers across which we could average. That still is not a completely straight forward way to proceed, because we immediately discover that no single reference point can anchor all items. Some items are missing for every particular time period. A more elaborate procedure is developed both to anchor by reference points when possible and then to leverage other information to build comparability across items when it is not.

The algorithm that does all this uses simple intuition but a good deal of tedious number crunching to accomplish the measurement goal. It is easy enough to illustrate the basic ideas, which I do here. Formal development of the algorithm is presented in Appendix 1. The illustration captures the spirit of the measure, except in one regard: that a very large number of series similarly processed brings plausibility to assumptions and reliability to measures well beyond the limited illustration.

To get a feeling for the intuition of this measurement methodology, let us begin with an example. This simplification uses only three series of preference marginals and only twenty-two years, 1975 to 1996. The three hypothetical (and, in fact, real) series are graphed in Figure 3.10a. Displayed in terms of the simple liberalism index (to be called the natural metric), the three lines are a combination of real values and interpolated

FIGURE 3.10a   Three Example Series, 1975–1996

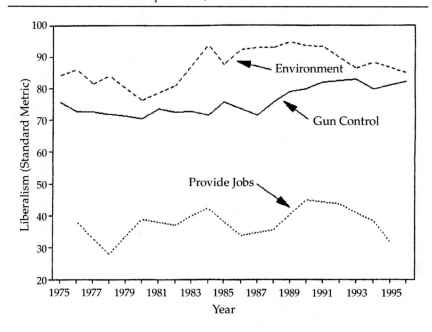

lines between actual administrations. Each is expressed in a metric determined by the particular wording of the question. None therefore is comparable to any other.

The twenty-two-year span presents every possible combination of item presence and absence, from all three for some years down to some years where none is present.[21] A basic first step is this: Although the natural metrics are not comparable, whatever the metric, ratios of measured values for any pair of years should be. Thus, for example, both for the guns and environment series, the 1995 values are about one percent larger than the 1996 values. That suggests that we can simply rescale the two series in terms of their final-year value, which we arbitrarily set to 1.0. Every other year for the two is then expressed as a ratio to its 1996 value. The data are presented again with this rescaling applied to the two series in Figure 3.10b. The two series are only slightly altered by a shift that brings together their final values. (The appearance is otherwise, however, a result of shifting vertical scale between figures, not real change.) That leaves them comparable, each annual value now interpretable as liberalism relative to the 1996 level. The third series remains in a metric (its scale shown on the right) not comparable to the other two. We can learn nothing from it as it stands.

FIGURE 3.10b   Three Example Series: Gun Control and Environment
Standardized by 1996 Values

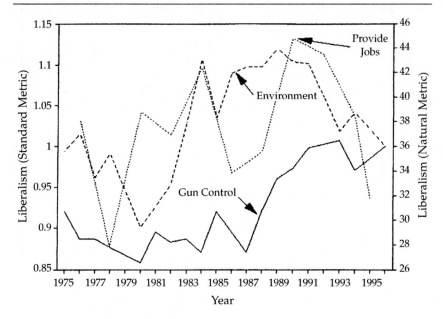

The trick now is to proceed to standardize the third series, even though
it lacks the common reference point of the other two. We cannot proceed
as before, choosing an arbitrary metric for, say, 1995, where all three series have measured values, because a second arbitrary metric would not
in general be comparable to the one already used. The solution in this
step is to take advantage of what we already know about 1995 from the
previous step. The best information we have is that the average of the
other series shows 1995 to be about 1.01 relative to the arbitrary 1.0 of
1996. We therefore use that best estimate to recompute all values of the
provide jobs series so as to produce that same 1.01 for 1995 on the provide jobs scale. Now a single common metric is imposed upon all three
series, and it is appropriate to find their (simple) average as an estimate
of their common tendencies over time.[22] The three series and their computed average are graphed again in Figure 3.10c.

The figure shows that the three series share some common movements—for example, the liberal low/conservative high around 1980—
and sometimes diverge in particular years. Where movement is common,
the mean series takes on striking values. Where it is not, the self-cancel-
lation tends to produce middling and moderate estimates of common
tendencies.

FIGURE 3.10c   Three Series in Standard Metric and Their Estimated Mean

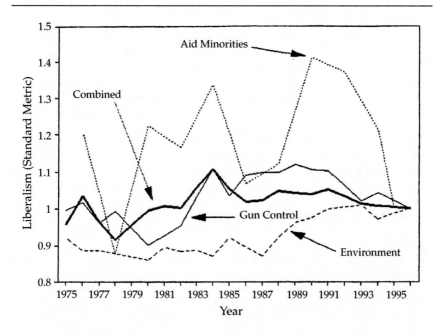

Implemented for over a hundred series instead of merely three, the problem involves prodigious number crunching. Its logic in the more complicated detail of Appendix 1 is basically that of the illustration, adding only one additional step, a means to weight issue series in proportion to their validity as indicators. Now we have a concept, policy mood, and more than one technology for measuring it. It's time to get to the thing itself.

NOTES

1. Such a consideration underlies the use of the normed liberalism index—Percent Liberal/(Percent Liberal + Percent Conservative)—as the basic measure, rather than one of its components alone. Subtle differences in filtering, including some not even discernible in question texts, tend to produce changes in the "don't know" categories relative to classifiable liberal or conservative responses. A single component measure (such as the "percentage conservative" of my earlier work) produces systematic error in the face of filtering change. To add a filter to a question where previously there was none, for example, would depress percentage conservative (along with percentage liberal) and produce a false measure of movement to the left. In the same situation the worst effect experienced by an index including both, in contrast, is an artifactual reduction in variance.

2. What comes closest to a standard, and the one I follow, is this: Percentages are calculated from the totals of all actual responses—every possible response from respondents to whom the question was actually administered. The "n.a." responses, typically associated with respondents who for one reason or another (interview terminated, second-wave sample mortality, and so forth) were never asked the question, do not count toward the totals.

3. When it isn't easy, for example, on issues of more or less international involvement, one gets some intuition on the boundaries of domestic policy mood. If the connection can't be coded with confidence, it probably doesn't exist.

4. A more difficult judgment call arises, if rarely, with in-between responses. Almost always these are coded as neutral and contribute nothing to the index values. In a couple of cases, on racial segregation, for example, a response like "leave things about the same as they are now" is pretty clearly a conservative option and is coded as such. All that matters is that such coding decisions be comparable over time.

5. From preliminary analyses foreign policy attitudes were known not to travel the same path over time as the domestic sphere and so are not seriously represented in the data.

6. Note that product moment correlations between items drawn from the same survey, as in these examples, are likely to overestimate the longitudinal associations. The problem is that the items will share some portion of their errors with other items in the same sample because each is subject to the same sampling fluctuation. If one randomly drew 1 percent too many liberals, for example, that error would be expected to inflate all measures of liberalism. Because sampling error is random with respect to time, that false association would be seen in year-to-year random fluctuations but not in patterns systemic with respect to time. It becomes trivial in analyses to come, where items are rarely drawn from the same samples.

7. The effects of wording loom very large in a refined time series analysis and are capable of producing considerably more systematic variation that the real change that is the target of study. Wording of questions must truly be consistent to produce the desired information, and this requisite causes unavoidable information loss when two versions of apparently the same issue have to be treated as different series with no a priori relationship. When the different forms don't overlap one another in time, the normal case, there is nothing to be done about it.

8. As a result, the 1950s and sometimes half of the 1960s will disappear from refined or disaggregated analyses to come because the necessary data don't exist. The long-term issues that never left American politics, the cluster conveniently called the New Deal agenda, go untapped during that period. In that period where we wrote about the "end of ideology" (Bell 1960), we did so with a conspicuous lack of measurement of the components of what was said to be ending.

9. When account is taken of a data matrix—issues by time—that has far more missing cells than measured values, principal components or similar models become swamped beyond believability by the estimation of unobserved values and the assumptions that must accompany the process. One common stopgap, analysis of a matrix of correlations computed with pair-wise missing-value assumptions, is also unworkable. Such a matrix cannot be constructed because many items have no overlapping cases with one another. Thus simple though it is in

concept, the consequences of missing observations preclude simple estimation of underlying tendency.

10. My motive is to convince the skeptical reader that the movements I will later extract can be seen in the marginals themselves, that the measurement algorithm to be later deployed refines them but does not create them.

11. Throughout this text, I use *all* to mean all that I can locate. Inasmuch as I continue to find fugitive items and series, it is clear that more exist that I have not yet found. Inasmuch as greater effort is expended locating fewer and fewer such fugitives, the number of those remaining to be found is not likely to be large.

12. The domestic policy category includes defense-spending issues and liberal and conservative self-identification, which, although relevant, is not a strict "policy" measure. The set does not include abortion measures, which follow a different track, or two "ends"-oriented measures of belief in equality for blacks and women. Depending upon which subset of years is considered, the number of distinct items is around 145. About 2,056 individual readings on those items form the domestic set.

13. Sullivan, Piereson, and Marcus (1978:246, table 6) demonstrate an "agree" response bias to the old format questions. Because agreeing is usually agreeing with a liberal change in government activity, the "agree" bias becomes a liberal bias.

14. These questions then become less reliable as time series as well because they are particularly sensitive to the context of the interview. It matters a great deal whether respondents are focused on problems in need of solutions or the cost of those solutions, and previous questions in the survey or last night's TV news might well have primed one or the other of them, so the marginals will be accordingly noisy as a time series. The better alternative forces respondents to consider both sides of the question and by providing its own priming—always the same—should produce a more reliable response.

15. This sort of specification was suggested by Chris Achen.

16. Taking the crucial assumption of representative values for each item, 3.1 is estimable from a linear regression of the form: $M = \beta Q + T\tau + U$, where M is a vector of all marginals, Q is a matrix of (number of items -1) dummy variables, each coded 1 if the current case is item i and 0 otherwise, and T is a similar matrix of time dummy variables. U is the usual regression error vector. The β vector we throw away; it serves its purpose by being estimated jointly with τ. The τ vector is a set of (number of years -1) offsets, each of which may be added to β_0 for an estimate of policy mood at time t for years 2 and after. β_0 itself estimates mood at year 1.

17. A more complicated model that might allow for estimated validities is available in the linear structural equations (sometimes called LISREL) tradition, but the complexity of ordinary least squares estimation for this problem is already daunting; a fully specified structural equation specification ratchets up complexity to the point where there is very little possibility that the right model *would* or could be estimated. For the vector notation of note 16 above hides the difficulty of the estimation problem, which comes from sheer numbers of variables and parameters. The regression for Figure 3.9, for example, requires estimation of 120 item parameters plus 40 time parameters plus an intercept. Written in

(conventional) scalar notation, the "little" equation would consume the better part of a page. Presented in tabular form, the reported coefficients would consume several (which is why Table 3.2 presents only goodness-of-fit criteria).

18. The Michigan election studies, the richest data resource of the time, illustrate the worst case. There the collinearity is perfect. None of the 1956–1960 policy items is continued after 1962, hence there is no possibility within the Michigan collection of separating real changes over time from changes due to format. Gallup items of the time, which continue later, partially salvage the situation.

19. Again the difficult assumption of representative missing values arises. Standardization presumes that we can estimate the mean and standard deviation of the whole series from the available portion, which may be atypical.

20. This as an assumption, not a fact, because the possibility does exist that changes in political context will produce differing responses to the same words at different times.

21. Values for four missing years are interpolated for this illustration to produce at least one measure for each year. This problem is specific to the illustration; it does not arise in full analyses.

22. The addition of ratios could mean trouble were variation extreme. But given basic preference stability and the calculation of ratios only between various administrations of the same item, variation is quite modest, mostly contained within the range of 0.85 to 1.15. Because the issue preferences are scaled as net differences between liberal and conservative preferences and then normed around 50, accidental variations from sampling and rounding can have only trivial effects.

4

The Components of Mood

Ideology won't go away. It is too important. For all its confusion and contradiction, we can't seem to do without it. And so, year by year, we talk about it, explain it. And we measure it. It can be measured. It often has been. Once we have put numbers on it, however, the problem is that we can't enforce agreement that these numbers are valid. Not a technical measurement problem, the problem is that we can't fully agree what ideology *means*. Scholar after scholar produces definitions, defines scales, builds measures. But none of them takes. Each lasts until the next exercise, which is then different on most counts.

We got some distance in the survey tradition by redirecting attention toward concepts that could be defined. "Belief system" (Converse 1964) is the notable achievement here. Clearly related to the confusing term that set off debate, belief system is a scientific concept. It can be defined in theoretical and operational terms that allow research that, however diverse or discrepant the findings, hones in on a consensual idea of what is to be investigated. Since Converse we've been able to set aside ideology and undertake research on belief systems.

Policy mood has something of the same character—or at least I hope that it does. It too shares much of its meaning with this messy ideology. But it is a scientific concept. And though not all concepts need measures to go with them, those that have them are generally a lot more satisfying than those that don't. Policy mood can be measured, can be, that is, assigned a set of numbers that indicate the underlying thing itself. That is the business of the moment.

The focus of this chapter is analysis—in its most literal meaning, the decomposition of whole into parts. I will briefly look at the product of all this development so far, the policy mood time series, and say something about how big and meaningful are its movements. Then I proceed to break the whole into parts, using the developed measurement system to create separate estimated moods specific to individual policy domains. The focus throughout is on how well the parts fit the whole and how well they fit one another. Two particular components, the idiosyncratic abortion issue domain and value-trade sorts of issue probes, get special attention at the end.

Estimating Policy Mood:
A Search for Political Eras

It's time to look at this measure, policy mood. For that purpose the dyadic algorithm is employed in Figure 4.1a on a set of 1610 readings on domestic issues (see Appendix 3 for item content).[1] The estimation is in two steps. First the algorithm produces estimates free of any assumptions about missing cases in the component series. That produces estimates that are basically well behaved and largely correspond (as they must) to patterns that can be seen in the raw marginals. The series has minor problems in one particular period, its first decade, 1952–1962, where the estimates show considerable year-to-year fluctuations not seen in the raw data.[2] The problem here is too few series for reliable estimation. Without the large numbers of series the method depends upon for reliability, minor changes in one or another series produce disproportionate impact on estimates. There are two means to eliminate this unreliable fluctuation.

FIGURE 4.1a   Estimated Policy Mood, 1956–1996: Original and Smoothed

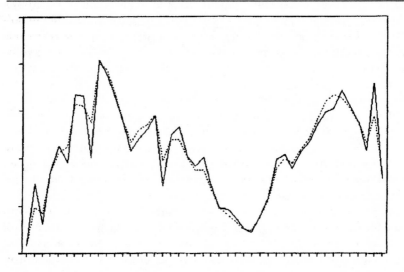

We can aggregate biennially, in which case nearly all that variation is eliminated when there are enough series overlapping in two-year intervals to produce reliable estimates. A two-year aggregation faithfully reproduces the long-term pattern.

It is useful, however, to retain the greater information in annual aggregation. A similar kind of smoothing can be gained by using our knowledge of random errors in survey samples. Although the survey estimates are the best information we have, we know that they err by a percent or two or three in the norm from sampling fluctuation. Where we have multiple independent samples for each period, as is the case for most of the period of analysis, then natural smoothing results from the process of averaging across random errors. But where analysis is based upon only a few samples, then the random fluctuations can make their way into the estimated series. We deal with this by implementing exponential smoothing during the iterative estimation—in effect smoothing over time when smoothing across issues is insufficient. This proceeds from the assumption that a smooth underlying transition is a better estimate of mood than the untamed year-to-year fluctuations induced by sampling fluctuation.

Both the unsmoothed original and the exponentially smoothed version are seen in Figure 4.1a. With a between-series correlation of .97, the two versions are almost identical at all times except the 1952–1962 period, where the smoothing has its intended effect. With fully aggregated data, as here, or a restricted time period, smoothing doesn't matter—isn't worth the trouble. But when we need to push the method into periods where data are thin or to estimate subsets of issues—as we do in this chapter—then the payoff is substantial.

Political Eras?

The picture of Figure 4.1a is worthy of a long look. It will be familiar from the patterns already seen in raw data. And it will be familiar as well to those who have commented upon differing political eras in American politics. It shows movement between periods of differing prevailing conceptions of government and politics, differing political eras. But it doesn't quite vindicate the pundits (or they it). A careful look at movements and dates will show that the movements uniformly precede the popular eras. It is clear in the figure, for example, that the liberal winds of the 1960s were blowing in the latter part of the *previous* decade, a gradual run-up that was gone soon after it was generally recognized to be in place.

The story of the 1980s is the same. If these estimates are to be trusted, the increasing conservatism of American life began in the mid-1970s, grew steadily, and was fully in place *before* the election of Ronald Reagan to the presidency. This strongly suggests that Reagan was beneficiary of a conservative mood, not due any credit for creating it. Because the movement away from conservative views begins almost with the Reagan inauguration, this suggests that the Great Communicator's talents at moving public opinion have been considerably oversold. The "revolution" that bears his name produced a more liberal American public than the one that elected him. There is a story to be told of the present and future here as well. I defer that to Chapter 6.

How liberal is liberal? How conservative is conservative? The scale of Figure 4.1a is determined by its individual items—it is a weighted average of them. Since each item may be interpreted to measure relative liberalism—scores over 50 indicate greater preference for activist government, those under 50 the reverse—so too a similar interpretation may be brought to the scale. If we interpret the scale to mean support for more or less government, then we may say that Americans at all times prefer more to less. The range of variation is between a rough balance at the "conservative" high points in the 1950s and 1980s and substantial majorities clamoring for more government at the liberal peaks. The early 1960s peak of about 70, for example, means that seven of every ten respondents who chose either "more" or "less" were on the "more" side. On this indicator, then, we may say that we have never experienced true conservatism—when pluralities would choose "less" over "more"—but rather only relative conservatism, when the normal majority favoring expanded government is checked.

Not all issue domains are equally involved in the global movements of Figure 4.1a. It is worth knowing which ones are, in order to get a handle on what the more general phenomenon encompasses. Some leverage on that issue is provided by Tables 4.1a and 4.1b, which present correlations between constituent items and the estimated latent mood for both the primary dimension and a statistically discernable second dimension. Tables 4.1a and 4.1b present the 25 items that contribute most substantially to each of the two dimensions.

An answer to what this primary underlying latent dimension taps comes fairly easily. The defining variables are essentially the New Deal issue cluster, with additions of race, environmental protection, and (opposition to) defense spending. The central issues have to do with how much the federal government should or should not do or spend in intruding itself into the domains of health, education, welfare, environment, and racial equality. There is no surprise here. This is what liberals and conservatives have argued about since the beginning of the New Deal. The domain is fairly strongly associated with items that tap crime and punishment and shows expected associations for other government responsibility issues, such as employment.

TABLE 4.1a Correlations of Issue Series with Estimated Mood: First
Dimension

Item	Survey House	Years	Product Moment Correlation
Taxes too high	Gallup	28	0.90
Spend on environment	GSS	23	0.91
Spend on urban problems	GSS	23	0.83
Spend on race	GSS	20	0.91
Spend on healthcare	GSS	23	0.74
Spend on education	GSS	23	0.70
Spend on welfare	GSS	23	0.62
Spend (less) on military	GSS	18	0.78
Gun control	Gallup	24	0.57
Education priority	Trendex	15	0.88
Bus for racial balance	NES	15	0.76
Fight inflation	Roper	14	0.81
Spend (less) on military	Gallup	17	0.66
Abortion legal	Gallup	14	0.74
Pay for medical care	GSS	12	0.84
Healthcare priority	GSS	17	0.59
Open housing	GSS	15	0.63
Government waste	NES	13	0.72
Spend on environment	GSS	11	0.82
Aid to minorities	GSS	16	0.56
Spend on race	GSS	11	0.76
Spend on healthcare	GSS	11	0.73
Government provide jobs	Trendex	16	0.50
Spend on education	GSS	11	0.73
Approve labor unions	Gallup	15	0.53

The secondary dimension (see Table 4.1b) lacks such a clean interpretation. If we take seriously popular commentaries, we would expect a
"social issues" dimension, defined by attitudes toward religious expression, social conformity, the public role in regulating sexual matters, and
the like. And the database includes numerous items on school prayer, ho-
mosexuality, abortion, birth control, and the like. The dimension that
emerges from the data instead points to crime and criminals on the one
hand, and the residual contributions of the same dimensions that define
mood on the other. The liberalism and conservatism of the first dimension, mood, are answers to the question, "How much should government
do?" The material of this second dimension seems to be more symbolic,
more the stuff of attitudes toward rich and poor, ins and outs. Unlike
mood, where liberalism is at its peak in the early Kennedy-Johnson years,

TABLE 4.1b   Correlations of Issue Series with Estimated Mood: Second Dimension

Item	Survey House	Years	Product Moment Correlation
Favor death penalty	GSS	22	0.78
Harsh treatment of criminals	GSS	24	0.56
Spend on healthcare	GSS	23	0.54
Privacy rights	Roper	14	0.85
Buyer protection	Roper	14	0.82
Government provide jobs	Trendex	16	0.70
Aid minorities	NES	13	0.84
Spend on welfare	GSS	11	0.96
Reduce income differences	GSS	15	0.70
Healthcare priority	GSS	17	0.58
Help poor	GSS	13	0.75
Taxes too high	Gallup	28	0.35
Favor death penalty	GSS	17	0.55
Education priority	Trendex	15	0.58
Spend (less) on military	GSS	18	0.44
Help minorities	GSS	12	0.62
Spend on healthcare	GSS	11	0.66
Aid to minorities	GSS	16	0.45
Approve labor unions	Gallup	15	0.46
Spend on welfare	GSS	23	0.29
Help solve problems	GSS	10	0.65
Government too big	NES	11	0.59
Big government	NY Times	7	0.91
Spend on environment	GSS	11	0.57
Affirmative action	NY Times	8	0.68

the second dimension grows steadily to a peak at the end of the Vietnam War in 1972. This suggests that the attitude sets identified as antiwar, counterculture, and, later, "Yuppie" (and equally opposition to them) are the defining materials. (But note that no measures of attitudes toward the war itself are included in the analysis.)

Is the recursive algorithm too "creative"? Or can the patterns it estimates be found equally with other methods, other assumptions? For a brief answer to those questions the recursive estimates are plotted against those produced by regression on standardized items from the last chapter. That gives us a feel for how these entirely different mathematical approaches converge or fail to converge.

Figure 4.1b shows both obvious similarities and some subtle differences. The similarities need little attention. The peaks and troughs are

FIGURE 4.1b   Two Estimation Techniques Compared

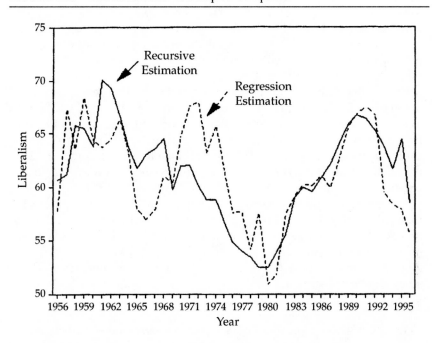

pretty much the same, as are most of the annual ups and downs. That is captured in a product moment correlation of .65. The dissimilarity reflects assumptions about validity. The regression method implicitly assumes equal and perfect validity; it gives equal weight to all series. The recursive method estimates the validity of individual series as a function of the variance that they share with the scale and weights them accordingly. The regression estimate is weighted not only by the first dimension, but also by the second, along with all variance associated with neither dimension. What we see in Figure 4.1b reflects that. The regression estimate shows liberalism peaking in the late 1960s and early 1970s, essentially an average of the two estimated dimensions. The crisper dimensional definition of the recursive approach is to be preferred.

The Scale of Attitude Change

Figure 4.1 falls short of demonstrating that the measured changes matter. For it is expressed in a partly artificial metric that doesn't readily allow one to discriminate large movements from small ones.[3] To get some perspective on the issue of scale, it is useful to work back to the sorts of survey marginals that produced the estimates and ask what the estimates imply for the raw data: large, moderate, or small changes over time.

A problem with doing so is that none of the original series comes close to spanning the full period for which it is possible to estimate the under-lying tendency. If one did, we could just translate estimated mood into the original metric and have a look. Because no such real series exists, we borrow the metric of a real series to create a hypothetical continuous se-ries over the period 1956 to 1996.

From Table 4.1a, it is clear that the Trendex "do more for education" item (and equally several others) differs from the estimated latent mood in little but measurement metric. With a product moment correlation be-tween the two of .88, there can be little but sampling error to differenti-ate them. We can't stretch this series, available for 1968 through 1982, but the next best thing is to create a hypothetical education series that is con-sistent with the real one and extends forward and backward in time.

The method is as follows. First we perform two regressions, predicting the percentage who say "do more" and then the (combined) "do the same or less." That produces coefficients in each case that allow the expression of mood in this real metric of survey marginals. That same metric then gives meaning to the latent variable over the whole time scale. That is what we see in Figure 4.2

FIGURE 4.2   Doing More for Education: Trendex Series and Hypothetical Projections, 1956–1996

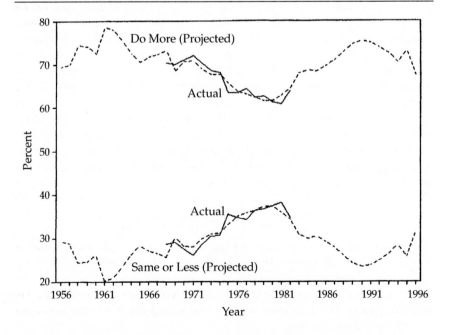

The figure presents the actual Trendex series, showing the percentage of respondents choosing the "more" and "same or less" options over time. Superimposed are two hypothetical education series, which are simply the mood variable reexpressed in the metric of the survey marginals. That allows the discussion of scale of change in terms of percentage responding, in terms of people.[4]

The actual series vary from a high of about 72 percent for the "more" option in 1971 to a low of about 61 percent in 1981. The spread is slightly more for the "same or less" responses, from a low of 26 percent in 1971 to a high of 38 percent in 1981. (This series is one of a small number of exceptions to the rule that series measured in 1980 have their most conservative value in that year.) The hypothetical series, because it exists for the more liberal early 1960s, varies more at the liberal end of the scale. The conservative extremes in 1981 are essentially the same as in the real scale. The high for "more" is 79 percent in 1963. The low point of the "less" response is 20 percent that same year. The variation for the period, high to low, is about seventeen points.

These are all of course "funny" numbers. But they give an impression of the scale of change associated with changing policy mood. Is a spread over time of seventeen points a large, medium, or small attitude shift? The answer depends a bit on prior expectations and a bit on how variable we expect sampled policy attitudes to be. In this case seventeen points was the difference between an extraordinary majority that demanded and supported new federal assistance to education in the 1960s and a lukewarm majority that watched Ronald Reagan dismantle much of it without much visible concern in the early 1980s.

In some areas seventeen points would be not much. Some foreign policy indicators are, for example, highly sensitive to presidential action, and a movement of that size there wouldn't amount to much. (But a similar exercise with such a variable issue would produce a bigger estimated spread.) On the extraordinarily stable abortion issue, on the other hand, a much smaller movement is rearranging the 1990s political landscape.

Part of an answer lies in the relationship of long term and short term. If a series moves a lot in the short term, large long-term changes are unimpressive. Short-term stability makes long-term movement look important. The largest annual movement in the actual Trendex series is 4.7 points (and the second largest a third of that). But part of that is systematic movement in the same direction as the series moves in the long term. An alternative estimate of the short term is to ask about movements in the "wrong" direction (i.e., away from the apparent drift), the zigs and zags of time series. The largest of those is a single point.

Ultimately there is an element of subjectivity in these judgments. The evidence of representational impact, showing policy change following shifting mood, would diminish the judgmental aspect if it is positive. We defer that issue to the final chapter.

Mood and Self-Identification

Both policy mood and self-identified liberalism or conservatism—the response to queries that ask respondents how they think of themselves—may be considered indicators of something like ideology. As such, they ought to be associated with one another over time. Where more people choose liberal policy options, more ought to consider themselves "liberal," for example. It is not quite that simple.

At least since Free and Cantril (1967) we have seen evidence that the ideological and operational aspects of attitudes are as often discrepant as joined. The abstract depictions of their worldviews that survey respondents choose, that is, seem to be almost wholly unrelated to the actual public policies they support or oppose. So large as to virtually determine any conclusion about the direction of public sentiment, the discrepancy is most apparent in the simple numbers of those willing to call themselves "liberals" vs. the numbers who consistently support liberal public policies. In a cross-section sample, the discrepancy, "so marked as to be almost schizoid,"[5] can paint liberals as an insignificant, even trivial, minority (ideological) or a large, even controlling, majority (operational). When we compare mood (the first, main dimension) in Figure 4.3 with the liberal proportion of the citizens who call themselves either liberal or conservative in various degrees, we see quickly that mood and self-identification have very different levels. Mood varies only in the liberal end of the spectrum, with about two out of three of those taking a position on policy choices adopting the liberal position. Self-identification is a wholly different story. It varies only in the conservative end of the spectrum, with about two out of three preferring the label "conservative" over "liberal."

It is tempting to ask, "Which is the real story, operational liberalism or symbolic conservatism?" The right answer is that both are real; most Americans *really* do prefer liberal policies, and they *really* do think of themselves as conservative. Any story that fails to embrace this contradiction fails to understand American politics. Not merely a matter of aggregation or a pattern that shows up only over time, this contradiction is deeply embedded in individual attitudes. If, for example, we made the seemingly harmless surmise that a survey respondent who attaches the label "conservative" to himself or herself would be likely to oppose increased spending on "liberal" domestic welfare-state programs, we would be wrong! The modal position of General Social Survey respondents who style themselves "conservatives" on six New Deal/Great

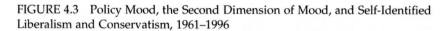

FIGURE 4.3 Policy Mood, the Second Dimension of Mood, and Self-Identified Liberalism and Conservatism, 1961–1996

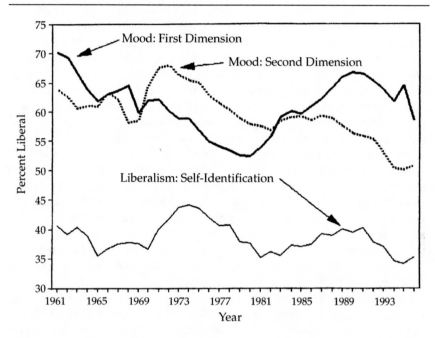

Society programs is one that advocates *more* spending (Erikson, Mackuen, and Stimson n.d.). While it is true that conservatives want to spend a little less than "moderates" or "liberals," it is also true that on balance they advocate a bigger government.

The Policy Components of Mood

The conceptual development to this point rests on an assumed *single*, latent dimension of policy attitude, mood. Issues that don't fit on it are presumed to have merely a specific character, rooted in the issue context. Abortion attitudes, for example, might be explained as a reaction to *Roe v. Wade* and ensuing public protests against it, not as part of any regular back and forth of American political life.

But it could be the case that the reality is "moods," plural, that several issue domains each have their own dynamic. Rather than one "mood" for all policies, might we not have one for economics, one for social welfare, one for church and state, one for tolerance of diversity, and on and on? Commentary assuming separate economic and social dimensions to politics is ubiquitous. And other such distinctions are reasonable.

If such were the case, it could be argued that the findings to this point are not a demonstration of "policy mood" but rather bits and pieces of the several dimensions of public thought, sometimes parallel to one another, sometimes not. This view would find favor with most of those who comment upon American politics. The argument is common that a single dimension such as liberal vs. conservative is a simplistic distortion of more complicated public views moving along several tracks.

How could we tell? It would be nice to know whether this popular view is also an accurate vision of public opinion. In concept, it always seems straightforward to employ some mathematical tool (such as principal components analysis) to make an exact determination. All who have done so have discovered that the neatness of the solution fades quickly with the kinds of complexity and confusion found in real data. Issues of dimensionality are never straightforward. And the answers to dimensionality questions are never automatic; what comes out is influenced to an uncomfortable degree by the analyst's assumptions and decisions that go in. And that is the case here as well. Asking about longitudinal dimensions—which comes down to the question of in-phase or out-of-phase—raises the same messy issues as the more common dimensional analyses of attitudes in a cross-section survey.

One means of attacking the dimensionality issue is simply to break up the various issue measures into sets that ought to go together. Then we can see if separate estimates for those sets run in parallel—more or less—or diverge over time. The various problems with survey marginals, in particular those associated with the nonrandom character of the decision to ask or not ask particular questions at particular times, complicate matters. Because the solution to those problems depends upon the leverage one can get from aggregating many items, any scheme for disaggregating into separate components loses that leverage. Reliable estimation depends upon knowing large numbers of item-to-item interrelationships over time.

The problems of missing data grow exponentially as the data are disaggregated. What is possible to tap with some reliability with a hundred or so flawed mini time series is not possible with a handful; the whole is considerably more reliable than its parts. Issue-domain comparisons become even more difficult where the components of different domains are central to public debate at different times. The available measures for each domain become, therefore, associated with both the density and quality of survey research of the era. Race, for example, is arguably separate (at some times) and arguably of central consequence (Carmines and Stimson 1989), but the lack of continuous measures of racial attitudes attenuates the possibility of observing a racial "dimension" that is more than a caricature of the issues as framed. What can be measured is recent responses to a surely atypical set of racial issues, and then only after the period where race was of central importance to American political life.[6] The registration of handguns, in contrast, is an issue for which good measures are abundant, a function of *when* the issue was contested much more than how central it is or was.

But those cautions aside, it is of some use to disaggregate into issue domains. Most importantly, it permits a look at separate sources of variation to see the degree to which they move together. Even if disaggregation is nothing like a satisfactory test of longitudinal dimensionality, one can nonetheless get some feeling for longitudinal dimensionality by separate measurement and side-by-side examination of components of the political agenda.

Before looking at some component series, we note two implications of the impact of disaggregation into policy components. First, time series will be available for reduced time spans. Estimates (for example, before 1964) that are difficult and less reliable for the full set of items are simply impossible for most components; the requisite item interrelationship does not exist. And second, even for the reduced spans the series are much less reliable than the full set. Much of the year-to-year variation in them is noise, the effects of small errors (particularly in sampling) that don't smooth out as they do in the full set by averaging across large numbers of items.

The Welfare State

Without a theory of which separate components to expect—for the analysts who agree that public opinion is multifaceted rarely concern themselves with the identification of the facets—the decisions on how to proceed are somewhat arbitrary. And they are to a large extent driven by data availability. I begin with a set of issue concerns arising from the New Deal and Great Society agenda. These are the mainline controversies over the extension of government to provide greater services in education, in health care, in welfare benefits for the needy, in solving the problems of the central cities, and in racial equality. They define the extension of the welfare state.

The question at hand is this: Do these represent five areas of controversy, each with its own dynamic of debate, event, controversy, and policy response? Or are they merely separate questions about policy debates that are different in principle but that in fact all turn out to be one? If different, we should expect to see systematically differing behavior over time. For the "events" in education would not be the same as those in welfare or health and so on. If instead they are merely alternate indicators of one concept, say, social welfare mood, then we expect their behavior, insofar as it has any systematic character, to run in parallel over time. Our first evidence on the point is seen in Figure 4.4a. With time series we can design figures to show communality (if not to produce it when it doesn't exist) or to highlight differences. Figure 4.4a is the first. Collapsing everything onto a common scale, it highlights parallelism—and makes it difficult to disentangle the components.

By any reasonable standard, Figure 4.4a shows parallelism. It shows a good deal of parallelism. (And if the noisy individual series were smoothed out with a moving average, it would show even more.) The two series (welfare and racial equality) that can be extended to 1964 reach relative high points then, just before the Johnson landslide election and the ensuing rush of the Great Society. All series move to the right shortly after the Great Society legislation was enacted. All reach relative highs again in the middle years of the Nixon administration, evidence that the much-frustrated Nixon had some reason to be frustrated: He was swimming against a heavy tide. All reach well into the conservative range around 1980. All rebound after. The question of whether or not they are parallel is easily settled. The remaining question is whether they have *any* distinctive character, whether they are patterned or random variations around a parallel central tendency. To answer that, we break them apart

FIGURE 4.4a   Five Components of the Welfare State on a Common Scale

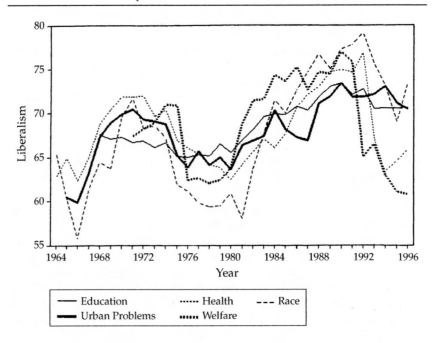

for individual analysis. Breaking them apart is accomplished by introducing artificial offsets between them, the effect of which is a flattening of the vertical scale and a diminished picture of parallelism. But in Figure 4.4b we can see the individual series as individuals.

The pattern of Figure 4.4b is three series (welfare, urban problems, race) that look to be nothing more than random fluctuations around a single parallel central tendency and two (education and health) that show some idiosyncratic behavior (along with basic parallelism). Education is a more universal value to Americans than are other components of the welfare state. Because this is so, the character of education debates is often different too, focusing less on the "do more/do less" aspect than on which levels of government ought to do more. With race, urban problems, and, to a lesser extent, welfare, the issue is often drawn between an activist federal government doing something vs. states, which, left to their own devices, will do nothing. In education states and localities act; no external imposition is necessary. The question then is often focused on which level of government ought to raise the revenue to permit pursuit of quality in public education.

Issues in health care are mainly parallel to other aspects of the welfare state. The difference arises from the surging liberalism preceding the

FIGURE 4.4b   Five Components of the Welfare State, with Artificial Vertical Offsets

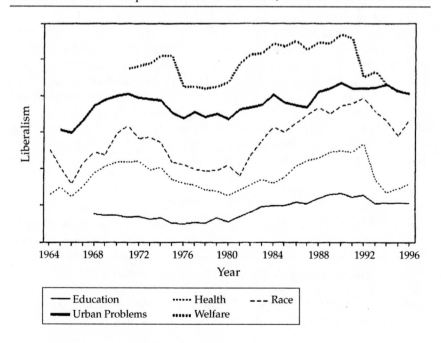

Clinton health care program of 1994 and the even more rapid decline following its legislative failure. Health care in a sense is the failure of the New Deal and Great Society agenda. Only the subsidiary issue of health care for the elderly got settled in the liberal direction of other programs. In the health domain the old, private, fee-for-service system with private provision of prepaid insurance is still the norm. But more and more Americans lack health insurance (in part the result of a declining industrial sector that provided such benefits in union contracts) and cannot pay for the care they need. The private health care provision and insurance system necessarily shifts the substantial costs of uncompensated care to those who do pay. This pushes premiums to painful levels and in turn causes more Americans to be uninsured. In an era during which other kinds of security are enhanced by programs such as unemployment compensation, food stamps, and deposit insurance, *insecurity* is growing rapidly in the health domain as a mounting proportion of ordinary Americans must come to grips with the knowledge that their only possibility of care when in need is to plead for free treatment. Inasmuch as this represents declining security between generations—the parents of many of those who now lack health benefits have (or had) them—one might expect a particularly pronounced political response. The (mainly young) people who now lack health insurance are of an age when they don't often need it. But as they age and parent children they face a worrisome future. Like inflation, which typically has tolerable current impacts but produces a fearful future, health insecurity might prove to be a powerful political brew.

Perhaps these stories of partially separate dynamics explain the normal parallelism and the limited divergence from it. Perhaps, too, they are after-the-fact rationalizations to the data as seen. But certainly before becoming too impressed with the partially separate paths of education and health, we ought to look back at Figure 4.4a to see just how partial that separation is. Both share most of their systematic movement with other aspects of the welfare state issue bundle. But the welfare state bundle itself is far from the whole of American political debate. We need to branch out from it to continue the query about separable dimensions.

Newer Concerns

I have followed the same strategy as before, looking first for evidence of parallelism and then for divergence, to estimate and plot four generally newer issue domains in Figure 4.5a. One, the controversy of the sheer size of the federal government, has much a priori communality with the welfare state issues. Three more diverse domains are crime—an amalgam of attitudes toward treatment of criminals and accused criminals and the related issues of handguns—military spending—which might either be a

FIGURE 4.5a   Size of Government, Crime, Military Spending, and
Environmental Protection on a Common Scale

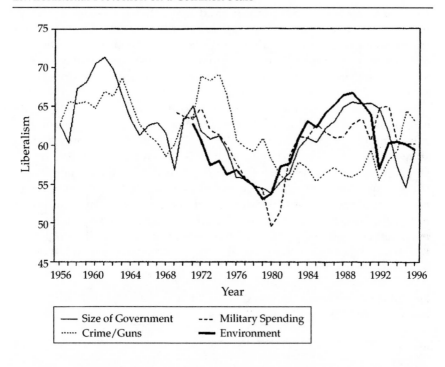

domain of values, order, discipline, patriotism, and so forth or simply the
reverse of preferences for domestic spending (Wlezien 1989)—and the environment. Unlike the welfare state issues, these latter three lack the common glue of sustained and consistent party positions over the long haul.
Virtually everyone wants less crime, a cleaner natural environment, and
ceteris paribus a strong national defense. Parties occasionally differ a bit
on many issues, but here the differences are subtle when they occur, and
they occur irregularly, unlike the welfare state controversies.

These controversies capture a diverse set of concerns and, excepting
abortion (see Figure 4.8), pretty much exhaust the kinds of issues that are
measured often enough and regularly enough to permit estimation of
common movements. Notably absent is something like "the social issue"
(Scammon and Wattenberg 1970). To attempt to measure such an issue is
to discover how ambiguous it is. In common use the concept seems to
imply anything that isn't a welfare state issue. But this catchall may be
popular mainly because of its convenience; it can mean anything you
want at the moment. That "it" means anything at all over the long haul
is probably a dubious proposition.

Figure 4.5a is a beginning look at the issue of parallelism of these diverse domains. For the 1970s and 1980s when all four series are available, the parallelism is quite strong. Pulled apart, the series don't diverge greatly from their combined look. Except for the expected flattening that suppresses evidence of parallelism, there is not much to see when the four are taken apart in Figure 4.5b that was not evident in Figure 4.5a. There is nothing here to indicate deviation from a single underlying mood.

Parallelism may be most notable, because it is least expected, in the case of military spending. Coded as the reverse of domestic spending issues ("more" is conservative, "less" liberal), this evidence would seem to show that response to the issue of more or less for national defense is a simple function of preferences to do more or less on the domestic side. "Spending" does not exhaust the potential issue domain of national defense, but it does exhaust the domain of good measures of defense attitudes. And other areas show that spending and value components track one another closely; where individuals might reasonably draw a distinction between whether the goals of a policy are good and whether we

FIGURE 4.5b   Size of Government, Crime, Military Spending, and Environmental Protection, with Artificial Vertical Offsets

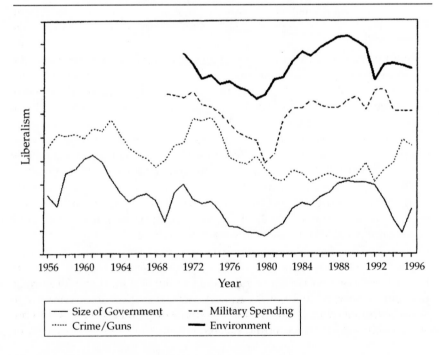

should spend more to achieve them, it is hard for aggregates over time to be "for" something and advocate spending less on it.

We can do better than talk about what does or does not "seem" to be parallel. Parallelism, after all, is correlation, moving together over time. Correlation can be measured. And sets of correlations between items can be analyzed, just as cross-sectional items would be, by dimensional tools such as principal components analysis. Once we have estimated continuous latent moods by domain, the missing-value issues that prevent use of such straightforward technology to the raw data are behind us, at least for a limited number of years.

A Principal Components Analysis

Starting with the nine latent series of Figures 4.4 and 4.5, we can construct a matrix of the correlations of every series with every other. The question to be asked, as before, is whether the set shows evidence of something in common, a common latent mood running through all and therefore accounting for their association. If there is such a common dimension, then we should be able to reconstruct much of the correlation matrix just by knowing about it. The task is to find such a dimension. The method is principal components analysis.

Principal components analysis reconstructs an observed set of n by n correlations by extracting n dimensions to (completely) account for them. The dimensions are extracted one at a time in such a way as to maximize ability to account for the observed matrix. The first is associated with all the variance shared by the set, the second with all the variance remaining after the first has claimed its share, and so forth.

Principal components analysis produces as many dimensions as there are series in the matrix—here, nine. But they are not of equal interest. Only a few will typically account for more variance than that of each series itself (by definition 1.0). The other, residual dimensions are a mop-up of everything that still remains. The task comes down to finding those "few" that matter. The analyst's task is deciding how many. The criterion is an "Eigenvalue," a measure of how much variance is associated with each dimension. Because each series contributes one unit of variance, the simple interpretation of the Eigenvalue is its ratio to the raw series, how much the dimension accounts for relative to how much each raw series accounts for.

An Eigenvalue less than 1.0 means that a "common" dimension explains less than the individual series (1.0) in the matrix; that is to say, it is *not* common. The remaining task, then, is to decide which of the dimensions with Eigenvalues greater than 1.0 (two of them here) are to be considered "common."[7] One visual means of doing so is the "scree" test. Its intuition is that if a dimension with an Eigenvalue greater than 1.0 looks like just a slightly larger version of the residual dimensions that follow it in the order of explanatory power, it probably is just that, a bigger residual dimension. If in contrast there is a sharp distinction, we are inclined to believe that it contains something systematic. In a display of Eigenvalues we look for an elbow, the point where there is a break between distinctive-looking common dimensions and the gently sloping decline of the residual dimensions.

The Eigenvalues are plotted in Figure 4.6. One is clearly a common dimension. Accounting for some 71 percent of the variance, the first dimension cuts across all of the nine domains. After that the drop-off is sharp, with a smallish second dimension only marginally larger than the third, the third only marginally larger than the fourth, and so on. The elbow, that is, comes after the first dimension of the solution.

If a dimension common to all series is present, principal components analysis will produce a strong first dimension with positive loadings (correlations of the series with the latent underlying dimension) for all items. That is the observed result. The first dimension, with an Eigenvalue of 5.73, accounts for 71 percent of *all* the association between the series. And it loads positively on all but the crime and civil liberties domain, with loadings ranging from .65 (crime) to .94 (race, size of government). Thus

FIGURE 4.6   A Scree (Elbow) Test of Dimensional Structure

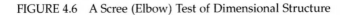

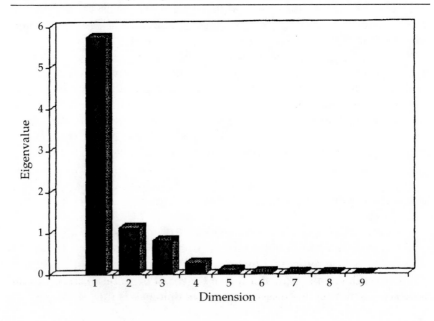

we have very strong evidence of parallelism and some ambivalence about whether there might be a second parallel track over time as well.

More can be learned by rotating the dimensional structure to clarify interpretation. Because the spatial orientation of the two-dimensional structure is not identified (the number of equally good ones, producing the same fit to the data, is infinite), we can gain some interpretive leverage by finding the one that produces the simplest pattern of loadings. The Varimax criterion, the goal of which is simple interpretation, is employed to this end, with the results seen in Table 4.2.[8]

Table 4.2, the loadings of the constituent series on the two tentative dimensions, shows pretty clear patterns for the first dimension and some confusion for the second. The first rotated dimension has strong positive loadings on six of the series. It looks like the concept policy mood. The second dimension in this solution is defined mainly by the crime and civil liberties issue domain.

Often the result of looking at such a rotated solution is seeing that those variables that define a secondary dimension have something in common. From that one infers the content of the dimension. But if I pose the question, "What do preferences about crime, punishment, and control of handguns (loading: 0.76) have to do with negative reactions to education (–0.86)?" the answer I come to is, "Almost nothing."

Part of the second-dimension issue can be resolved by looking at how the two estimated dimensions track over time. "Factor scores," estimated

TABLE 4.2   Nine Independent Policy Domains: Factor Loadings with Varimax Rotation

	Dimension	
Domain	*Mood*	*?*
Education	.39	–.86
Health	.76	–.39
Race	.73	–.61
Urban problems	.70	–.43
Welfare	.35	–.59
Size of government	.83	–.47
Crime, guns, civil liberties	.36	.76
Military spending	–.84	.23
Environmental protection	.54	–.70
Eigenvalue	5.73	1.12
Percent of variance	70.8	13.8

Note: Table entries are loadings—interpretable as correlations—of the nine independently estimated series with the two dimensions derived from them.

FIGURE 4.7   Two Dimensions of Mood and Two Principal Component
Estimates

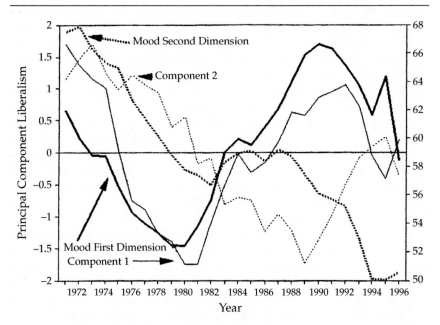

from the known association of the raw series with the latent dimensions,
produce estimates of the two dimensions, graphed together in Figure 4.7.
Also in the figure are the two dimensions of mood from the earlier Figure
4.3. We can ask whether this common component, which was extracted
from nine domains, is the same dimension as mood, and the answer
clearly is that it is. For the period where both are available, mood and the
first principal component correlate at .75. And the figure tells the same
story; these two alternate estimates, derived from wholly different approaches—the solid lines in the figure—trace the same dynamic.

   The two estimates of a second dimension of public preference—the
dotted lines in the figure—are, as always, less clear-cut. They map the
same liberal-to-conservative trend up through the early 1980s but then
diverge notably after that. This failure to converge is consistent with an
interpretation of the second dimension as a residual of systematic variation that does not move with the common first dimension.

Abortion: A Domain by Itself?

Abortion is exceptional. This issue, subject of such heated contest in the
years before—but especially after—the contentious *Roe v. Wade* decision

of the U.S. Supreme Court, moves alone. It shares its dynamics (if indeed it has any) with no other issue domain. Perhaps it is out of phase with other issue tracks. If one looks hard enough at Figure 4.8, a lagging phase relationship can be seen. (But the eye and the imagination could probably find "phase relationships" among series of drifting random numbers as well; we are a bit too creative in that regard.) Perhaps abortion is simply unrelated to all other issues, period.

Abortion preferences are unusual time series. Compared to all others their variation is small. After a jump associated with the *Roe v. Wade* decision, the central tendency of abortion attitudes is about the same year after year. That constancy is definitely not the result of averaging meaningless variations (which could tend to produce the same central tendency over time). To look at the individual abortion items, which are numerous and of good quality, is to see series, each of which is almost flat. But when the individual series move by a point or two, they move in tandem.[9]

If we start with the normal presumption that issues are independent of one another, this is not a finding. Having seen that all other issues move together, we note with interest that one does not follow the common path. Why should this be the case for this one issue and not for others? Perhaps the exception has something to tell us about the norm. What would seem

FIGURE 4.8   Mood and Abortion Attitudes

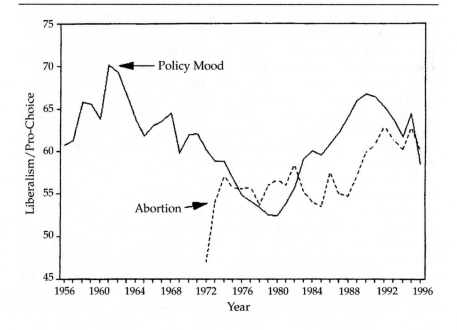

to be special for this one issue is the degree to which people talk about it and think about it in its own terms. After the glow of editorial-page preaching about government dies down, the truth about most political issues is that they do *not* matter much in people's everyday lives. They undoubtedly have impacts, but the distance between government and everyday life is so great that one needs to be a policy analyst to find those impacts. Programs are born, implemented, incremented, and die without ever derailing many people from their normal routines. They are just too distant.

Abortion is not distant. Perhaps no other activity of civil government can be more direct or intrusive. If many decisions along the way change our lives, the decision whether to have a child is one known in advance to be a big one. Unwanted pregnancy often brings women to critical decision points from which there is no return. Stay in school or drop out, get married or don't get married, pursue a career in the work force or compromise it to raise children? These are big, obvious decisions. In a society where abortion is legal, it will be chosen often, considered even more often. It becomes hard to imagine a woman of child-bearing age (or the parents or the mate of one) not thinking about abortion as a public issue. If it is the chosen option, then government threats to restrict it loom ominously. If it is rejected, that rejection might carry a strong value orientation for whether or not others should have the choice.

Where issues are remote, their effects indirect, ignorance of actual government policies is ubiquitous. I suspect that most people—even teenagers, in whom ignorance about politics often reaches its zenith— know the basic policy about abortion.[10] Other issues can track together because ordinary people pay little attention to issue debates. The cognitive miser takes no position at all or adopts the standard liberal or conservative views as his or her own. In abortion, people think about the issue in its own terms, come to their own conclusions.

A macro-level explanation may also give some leverage, both for this case and the norm. One characteristic of the history of the abortion controversy is that it cuts across party lines. Where party lines help to inform and reinforce ideological divisions, crosscutting issues produce confusion. The earliest abortion advocates were drawn from the educated upper-middle class, a group of nominally Republican sympathy. The strongest opponents were drawn from two religious groups, Catholics and (later) evangelical Protestants,[11] both with historic ties to the Democrats. At least before the 1980s, abortion was fought out more within party lines than across them. Perhaps—and it is too soon to say anything stronger—this ceased to be the case in the 1980s. With the coming of Reagan, the open disavowal of an historic commitment to women's rights by the 1980 GOP convention, and the courtship of conservative

Catholics and evangelical Protestants, an issue evolution (Carmines and Stimson 1989; Adams 1997) may be in its early stages. In the first edition of this book, I concluded that it was too soon to say. But if one looks at the *new* data of Figure 4.8—the period after 1989—one sees mood (liberalism) and abortion (pro-choice) running nicely in tandem. With these data in hand, I concur with Adams (1997) that we are witnessing an issue evolution. That predicts a future in which *liberal* will come to mean *pro-choice, conservative* to mean *pro-life*, and vice versa.

Values and Priorities

The discussion to this point assumes that the relevant lines along which to disaggregate the raw materials of survey marginals are those between domains of content. The distinctions are of *what* the questions ask. The categories have been wholly exclusive, no one series allowed to count in more than one domain. But in a final look at the pieces of mood, I turn the focus to *how* the questions were asked. That involves putting all the filling back into the pie and slicing anew along different lines.

The format of survey items we know matters. One major difference in the way policy preferences are ascertained is in whether respondents are asked explicitly single-valued questions—should the government do more about education? spend more on defense? and so forth—or probed by queries that force a choice between competing values—punish criminals or protect the rights of the accused, promote employment for all who seek to work or let individuals get by on their own? The "do more/do less" kinds of questions tap priorities. They seem to require implicit value trade-offs; governments that do less tax (or borrow) less and intrude less. But the survey respondent forced to choose explicitly must trade off alternative values, whereas the same respondent answering a "do more/spend more" query *might*.

The critical question to be posed here is this: What if the entire evidence of mood is produced not by genuine causation from the global (mood) to the specific (policy preference) but rather because large numbers of respondents are responding to "do more" itself as the issue? Just because professional students of public policy agree that, say, education and health care are separate domains doesn't mean that typical citizens will also make that distinction. If citizens see doing more or less as the issue, without regard to "in what?" then we would have something akin to Fenno's (1966) "budgetary moods." And though that is still a global mood worth study, it carries much less ideological baggage than a mood that goes beyond more or less government.

We already have in hand some evidence, the longitudinal trade-off between domestic and military spending, that suggests that more or less spending itself is *not* the central issue. If just preferences for more or less spending drove everything, then we should see a positive, not trade-off, relationship between guns and butter. Respondents should advocate doing more in both at the same time, not sacrificing one to promote the other. To balance guns against butter is to assert priorities, and that is something more than willingness or unwillingness to open the federal purse.

We can get a different sort of leverage on the question by treating the style of question as a meaningful division point and asking if we then estimate the same mood with different styles. Some measurement difficulties impede a clean comparison. Chief among them is that there are many fewer trade-off sorts of series. And they, in turn, are concentrated in the National Election Studies, which (1) did not adopt the question style until 1964 (and not with consistent batteries of questions until 1970) and (2) then occur only every second year. The best series of the items that can be assembled is thus biennial—and even then only for the period since 1961–1962—reliably for less than that.

Do we then see the same or different pictures of mood when question styles are segregated? One could come to either answer from Figure 4.9.

FIGURE 4.9   Two Kinds of Issues: "Do More/Do Less" Priorities vs. Value Trade-offs

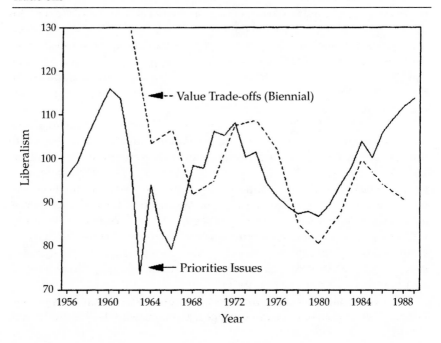

Part of what the figure shows is true, the general shapes of movement of the two series over time. And part, the greater apparent variability of the value trade-offs, is illusion; the series is just a less reliable instrument because it is based upon much thinner materials. And its two-year movements (with in-between points interpolated to produce a continuous line) look starker than the annual "do more" series. The substantial early differentials in particular should not be given much weight; they actually show the same monotonic variation in both series, differing from shifts in scale.

The divergence of the two sorts of series in the latter 1980s is another matter. In this case there is no particular problem with the data, and so the divergence might be telling a story of genuine differences. The time span is too limited (particularly when one of the series is measured only at two-year intervals) for a strong inference, but this is akin to a divergence we have seen before, first in self-identification and again in the second principal component estimate of mood (driven chiefly by concerns of law and order). It is a repeat of a sharp reassertion of preferences for a larger domestic role for the federal government that is not wholly parallel with a more symbolic and value-laden liberal vs. conservative dialog.

This, in a sense, is the end of the story for a limited conception of policy mood. We have seen that it exists. Within the limits of the data and the measurement technology, we have seen that it can be broken into separate pieces and that those pieces usually—but not always—look much like the whole. If the question is restricted to the simple "Do things go together?" the answer is equally simple: yes. For at least the public opinion side of public policy studies (never a particularly prominent portion of that genre), this is a strikingly subversive conclusion. It suggests that the starting assumption, that policies can be best understood by a focus on their uniqueness, is wrong. With few exceptions, what one gets by focus on the specific, not already known from the general, is errors in measurement and sampling fluctuations. This is a portrait of a macro public that derives specific preferences from global attitudes, top down, not one that builds global attitudes from the starting point of specific preferences,[12] bottom up.

Yet to be determined is how much any of this matters. And most of that question lies beyond the bounds of this essay, if not beyond the bounds of knowing. But one little piece of "does it matter?" is whether it matters for election outcomes, the topic to which we turn in Chapter 5.

NOTES

1. The set excludes abortion, military spending, and self-identified ideology. Relationships to each of those domains are taken up later in the chapter.

2. The year 1960 is particularly problematic. In a period where only the Michigan election studies produced policy preference measures at regular intervals (Gallup measures were sometimes frequent but always irregular), 1960 was the final use of "old" format preference items in the election studies. The format change has very large consequences for the marginals, which simply have to be treated as different series. The backwards recursion method thus has no later series with which to connect the Michigan items. (And use of a forward alternative would simply shift the problem to 1964.)

3. A note on graphic conventions: Page and Shapiro (1989), citing Tufte (1983), argue that any display of the marginal percentages of survey responses with less than the full 0–100 percent range of possible outcomes produces an illusion of change greater than the reality. Although I won't often display such marginal percentages, I will not follow the Tufte convention when I do. The Tufte prescription has a big problem of its own, an illusion of no change in marginals time series where real change is present. We are more often wrong, I will argue, in concluding that public opinion does *not* change (when it truly does) than in concluding that it does (when it truly doesn't). Thus I adopt the graphic convention most robust against the greater threat. Collapsing presentation to the real range of variation (instead of the larger potential range) does highlight change. But evidence for the critical inference, *that the change is real,* must arise from covarying series. Scale cannot produce covariance. Indeed, a reduced scale of presentation where covariance is absent makes change look large *and random.*

4. The two are not exact mirror images because of changes in the "don't know" responses over time. But they are very close to it. Both are presented to get closer to the typical presentation of survey marginals.

5. The quotation is repeated from Schlesinger (1986:249).

6. The case is worse yet for the presumed central conflict along the lines of labor vs. management, which had its day on center stage largely at a time when surveys were much less abundant than now and survey researchers evidently regarded repeating a previously posed item as showing a lack of imagination.

7. The issue is a bit more complicated, unfortunately less objective, than just choosing as many dimensions as have Eigenvalues greater than 1.0, because secondary dimensions are typically extracted that meet this criterion from the chance association of the individual series. The difficult decision for these secondary dimensions is whether they tap common structure or common errors.

8. More specifically, the Varimax criterion attempts to maximize the location of variables on either one or another dimension, rather than having them more weakly associated with several. Correlation between variables and dimensions is constant, but rotation of the dimensional space has the effect of reallocating that total association from one to another dimension. There are no better or worse solutions; they are all mathematically equivalent. But there are solutions that are more interpretable or less interpretable. The goal then is to choose from between those equivalent solutions the one that is most readily interpretable.

9. I am always aware of, and therefore discount, parallel movements that could arise from sampling error where two series are derived from the same samples, as is the case with several abortion items in the General Social Survey. Parallel movement is also seen in independent samples.

10. A *New York Times*/CBS News survey of July 25–30, 1989, gives some support for the assertion. Following the Supreme Court's *Webster* decision, 37 percent of respondents were willing to express an opinion about that specific decision (not just abortion in general). The other 63 percent said that they didn't know enough about it (59 percent) or didn't answer (4 percent). Of the 37 percent with opinions, 29 percent correctly interpreted the decision as one that gave states more power to restrict abortions; 2 percent over-interpreted its effect as making abortion illegal under most conditions; 5 percent got it wrong, saying that it imposed fewer restrictions; and another 2 percent didn't answer a follow-up asking what the decision did. In a context of generalized ignorance of virtually all political facts, those are impressively high numbers.

11. Because we constantly err in thinking the past was more like the present than it was, it is worth recalling that in the time before *Roe v. Wade*, when abortion was a state issue, some of the more permissive abortion laws were found in the South. The presumed reason at that time was that abortion divided Catholics from Protestants, and there were few Catholics in the South. The rise of activist opposition to abortion among evangelical Protestants is a more recent phenomenon.

12. The aggregate data do not permit an inference that individuals also function global to specific. But neither are they inconsistent with it.

5

An Electoral Connection?

George McGovern was defeated in South Dakota. Frank Church went down in Idaho. That one November day in 1980 Gaylord Nelson fell in Wisconsin, Birch Bayh in Indiana, John Culver in Iowa, and Warren Magnusen in Washington. Liberals all, their challengers were mainly conservative, some unusually so. Twelve Democratic seats fell that day, the party not merely decimated but twice-decimated. And this was in one election, where only one of three seats was at stake. Elections for the U.S. Senate are not usually like this. In the years since their last big win in 1958, the Democrats had gained in ones and twos and threes. And then they lost twelve at a shot. They lost the Senate. They lost the White House. They held the House of Representatives but suffered their largest losses there since 1966. When the survivors reassembled in January of 1981 for the State of the Union from a new conservative Republican president, they were scared. They had seen a message.

More than just an election outcome—for that, after all, was over—the surviving Democrats of 1981 saw a change in national mood. They saw it more clearly than the rest of us. Their stake was higher. They saw a Ronald Reagan pumped to heroic proportions not just by the election but by the election and a sense that the people had spoken. The survivors whose jobs had been on the line in 1980 had won them. But their wins came with a sense of foreboding about the future. They had seen some of their voters turned to the right. Close to the ground, as successful elected politicians must be, they had seen new doubts, eroding loyalties, vulnerabilities supplanting strengths. And what they saw changed them. And that changed public policy.

This chapter is about the electoral consequences of mood. It explores how mood alters outcomes of elections for the presidency and Congress. And then it attempts to reformulate an old idea, that election results might sometimes be mandates for policy change.

Public Opinion, Elections, Outcomes

When one discusses public opinion in American politics, often it is in the context of public opinion *and elections*. Public opinion gets its influence because it moves election outcomes, and through them public policy. I wish to begin treatment of electoral effects of mood cycles with a small dissent from that position. The assumption that elections must mediate mass views and policy response is so common that we easily overlook other mechanisms that might achieve the same effect.

This view of elections as mediators has a problem. To work well it requires politicians to be neither smart nor knowledgeable. What politicians must do to make the mechanism work is to pursue policies that they know to be out of favor with the electorate in order to provide the latter with an opportunity to send a message saying so in the next election. Or else they must be insensitive, letting public views change without noticing it.

Nothing we know about elected politicians in the big-time national game is consistent with assumptions that they are either dumb or insensitive to public opinion. If perhaps we don't quite "know" the contrary, that they are typically both savvy and sensitive to the movement of opinion, it is at least a much more plausible assumption to make. And all agree that the ambition to be elected and reelected is usually present in pretty strong measure.

How might ambitious, savvy, and opinion-sensitive politicians behave with respect to changing public preference? By assumption they would sense the change. And then it seems likely that they would undertake subtle alterations of behavior to position themselves to maximize their goals with respect to the changed context. They would not change positions from one side to the other. Neither the strategic imperative of maintaining a decent level of consistency nor their own personal values would permit flip-flops.

But there are many in-between strategies. Few observations of political behavior are more common than that of the "trimming of sails," politicians sensing that their positions are out of favor and de-emphasizing them. They can simply stop talking about unpopular issue position A and put new emphasis on B. Or, if my earlier analyses are correct, that any two A and B, both domestic issues, will be moving in parallel, they can focus their political attention elsewhere, appealing to common values, emphasizing performance (their own or the opposition's), or whatever. In these ways policy actors can in effect go underground, maintaining their views but moving attention away from them. That is only the negative side. We also expect those whose positions are gaining public support to be activated. One wants to be out front, after all, when there is a decent assurance that the crowd is following.

Such behaviors systematically practiced will have the effect of denying the electorate easy choices through which it can express changed preferences. And at the same time those behaviors may be consequential for policy outcomes. Trimmed sails may aid political survival, but they don't make effective policy advocates. The side not trimming is more likely to prevail. Changing public views thus might get represented in changing policy without ever being expressed in election returns. All that requires is politicians smart enough to anticipate the near electoral future.

What, then, should we expect about policy moods and elections? I am agnostic. Effects might be there to be found and might not. It isn't a trivial matter to know or not know. For we always seek more leverage in the explanation of election outcomes. But neither is it decisive for the concept of policy mood that it does or doesn't provide explanatory leverage on elections.

Policy Mood and Partisanship

Before looking at elections themselves, we examine macropartisanship, the aggregate of party identification over time (MacKuen, Erikson, and Stimson 1989). Because this aggregate is the central concept of individual-level analyses of electoral behavior in America, we entertain the suspicion that it also moves election outcomes. It ought, in particular, to follow phenomena such as policy mood that are relatively current responses to the changing context of politics. Macropartisanship is part habit, part unquestioned loyalty, part standing decision. All these suggest inertial dynamics, that cause into effect should be a process that works itself out over time. The standing decisions of an earlier day we expect to resist and delay but *not* finally to prevent the causal influence of changing policy views.

A macropartisanship time series is constructed using the same technology for combining series as for mood.[1] The combined result of twenty-three variations on survey house and question format and 2,010 raw marginals, the resulting series is very well behaved, very highly correlated with its constituent series, which are very highly correlated among themselves.

Mood and macropartisanship, graphed together in Figure 5.1, suggest a perplexing non-relationship. Although occasional periods of covariation can be found in Figure 5.1, the statistical evidence denies any permanent relationship. It is reasonable to expect preferences and attachments to the parties that represent preferences to move together. But they do not. I can explain why they ought to be related. But I cannot account for why they are not.[2]

For elections themselves, we turn first to the presidency. Presidential elections ought to be the cleanest case. The link between policy and party

FIGURE 5.1   Mood and Macropartisanship

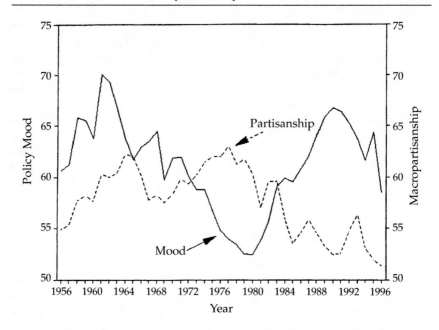

has always been a muddled one. But it is probably least so in presidential elections, where Democratic candidates have always been more liberal, if by varying degree, than Republican opponents. And, too, presidential candidates are much less free to hide their positions than are other actors. They get too much attention to control the way they are seen, which less visible actors can do.

Presidential Elections

Election results are independent phenomena from the concept of policy mood. Mood is based upon policy preferences and nothing else. In particular it has no partisan content except the empirical association of views with parties. Parties and elections are no part of its definition.

For popular conceptions of moods and political eras the reverse is the case. We come to think of eras as liberal or conservative in part from the way liberal and conservative *candidates* fare in elections, particularly presidential elections. It would be very difficult to separate 1960s liberalism from Lyndon Johnson's 1964 landslide victory over Barry Goldwater. And talk of a new conservative era began in earnest from the day in November 1980 when Jimmy Carter, the incumbent president seeking a second term and representing the majority party, was vanquished by Ronald Reagan.

Because we have seen that policy mood has much in common with popular beliefs about eras, it should not be surprising then to see some evidence of a link to presidential election outcomes. We start with a casual look at that evidence in Figure 5.2, which plots the Democratic percentage of the (two-party) popular vote from 1956 to 1996. The bars in the graph are election outcomes, labeled with the names of winning and losing candidates. The line in the background is the now familiar mood series, estimated biennially.

The figure provides some suggestive evidence for a connection between mood and outcome.[3] The fit would be reasonably strong were it not for 1976, when the Democrats nonetheless nominated their most conservative choice of the postwar period, and for 1980, a Democratic electoral disaster that doesn't look like one in simple terms of percentage.[4]

Pictures like Figure 5.2 can give impressions. But they can convey illusions as well. The issue of connection needs more refined analysis. And it needs to be expressed in a plausible model of election outcomes, which are driven by many factors in addition to this one possibility, mood. We need to model those factors, but with eleven cases, specification issues get dicey. The tiny sample makes it very hard to achieve statistical signifi-

FIGURE 5.2   Democratic Percentage of the Two-Party Popular Vote in Presidential Elections and Policy Mood

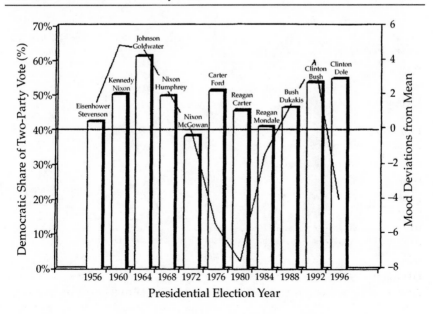

cance, which depends on sample size. And at the same time it makes it uncomfortably easy to cheat by trying out models until, with any kind of luck, one works for the hypothesis at issue. The danger of the latter is less author lying to reader than author lying to both self and reader. The cheating can be inadvertent. It is useful in this context to begin with bivariate results, which have the one virtue of not having been "tried out"; they are what they are.

The bivariate regression is seen in the first column of Table 5.1. The mixed result we have seen continues in the regression. On the one hand the regression coefficient (0.42) models a very strong effect. The twelve-point swing in mood between the 1964 liberal high and the 1980 low translates into a $12 \times 0.42 = 5.0$ percent difference in the two outcomes, out of a sixteen-point total swing. That is a huge effect. But with only eleven cases, the fit that goes with that huge effect is poor. The regression explains much but not well. And it also fails to be significant. If we had to stop here, the evidence would be confounding.

Presidential elections are partisan elections. Macropartisanship, a measure of net partisan sentiment—here, the aggregate of party identification for election years and the preceding year—is therefore introduced to account for this variation, which has nothing to do with policy mood. Macropartisanship picks up the effects of long-term commitments, and it

TABLE 5.1   Democratic Percentage of the Two-Party Presidential Vote, 1956–1996

	(1) Mood Alone	(2) Party Added	(3) Party and Incumbency
Variable			
Policy Mood[a]	0.42	0.52	0.84
	(0.52)	(0.56)	(0.41)
Incumbency[b]			6.16
			(2.02)
Democratic		0.43	0.20
macropartisanship[c]		(0.68)	(0.48)
Intercept	23.14	−7.45	−13.10
	(31.82)	(58.83)	(41.23)
R^2	.07	.11	.62
R^2 (adjusted)	−.04	−.11	.46
N	11	11	11

[a] Biennial estimate: The value for the election year and the preceding (odd-numbered) year is used.

[b] Effects dummy: Coded 1 if Democratic incumbent, −1 if Republican incumbent, 0 otherwise.

[c] Democratic percentage of national (two-party) party identification.

is handy for this analysis, where each degree of freedom is precious, because it also is known to incorporate the effects of presidential approval and the state of the domestic economy (MacKuen, Erikson, and Stimson 1989).

Model 2 of Table 5.1 introduces partisanship into the prediction along with mood. The result is an equation in which neither variable is now significant[5] and the equation fit is poor. The effect of policy mood does not diminish with another explanatory variable present but instead strengthens to 0.52, now implying a maximum contribution of more than six points. That is a great deal; adding or subtracting that contribution could have reversed all but two of these eleven elections.

For a final specification we add a routine phenomenon of American presidential elections, our tendency to give first-term presidents a second term. That is not a particularly interesting theoretical effect, but it is hard to question that it is a real one. That produces the third, "fully" specified,[6] model. The incumbency effect is coded to predict that being an incumbent helps the incumbent's party, hence for this regression, where the Democratic vote is dependent, it is scored –1 for Republican incumbents, +1 for Democrats, and 0 where no incumbent is seeking a second term.[7]

In model 3 the incumbency effect can hardly fail. For even though two incumbents lost (in 1980 and 1992), the four largest electoral margins of the period (1956, 1964, 1972, 1984) are for incumbents seeking second terms. What happens when incumbency enters the model is that it diminishes the explanatory power of partisanship but actually increases the effect of policy mood (now reliably estimated in the better-fitting model: $t = 2.05$, $p = .04$). The reason mood holds its explanatory power, in spite of competing with incumbency to explain, for example, 1964, is that mood and incumbency offset one another to succeed in predicting the 1980 and 1996 results, where either one alone fails. Incumbency and party advantage predict easy wins by Carter over Reagan in 1980 and by Bush over Clinton in 1992. It takes mood to account for the success of the conservative challenger in conservative 1980 and the liberal challenger in liberal 1992.

What is the state of the evidence from these regressions? This is a plausible statistical model of American presidential contests. But others are too. And policy mood doesn't perform well uniformly; nothing can with eleven cases. But when it doesn't, it is usually the case that the magnitude of the coefficient is in the same range, that is to say, predicting substantial impact, but with unacceptably large standard errors from ill-fitting specifications. For example, adding change in disposable income[8] (often employed as a measure of government economic performance) results in an overall decrement in model performance, with income insignificant in the wrong direction and the mood coefficient increased, but with a large standard error that deprives it of significance.

One way to tease out the potential danger of so few degrees of freedom is to ask whether the coefficients depend disproportionately upon particular cases for success. That is addressed here by estimating the full model eleven successive times, each time leaving out a particular election, to see whether the coefficients are stable. All of the coefficients are sensitive in so small a sample. They bounce up and down and move in and out of the significant range. The mood coefficient is the most stable of the three.

The coefficient is quite uniform, never lower than about .6, never higher than about 1.1. A parameter estimate may be the result of relatively uniform behavior or it may be the average of one or two spectacular "hits," where most cases are "misses." Uniform behavior we need to take seriously as evidence of a structured relationship. That is what we see here.

Presidential Elections as State Contests

The U.S. Constitution and two hundred years of convention establish presidential elections as state-by-state, winner-take-all contests. Although the difference between the national and state outcomes may often be overemphasized, the possibility of difference is undeniable. Thus to know that mood seems to move the national aggregate outcomes doesn't quite clinch the point of the state contests for electoral votes, a slightly different matter.

The states also present a statistical opportunity: The mere eleven data points for national presidential elections from which it is so hard to squeeze meaning become eleven data points for each American state. Pooling the state contests into a larger sample of eleven (elections) by forty-seven (states) provides the analytic leverage the national outcome lacks.[9]

The regressions of Table 5.2 are roughly parallel to those we have just seen with the national popular vote data. Here we explain the state-by-state popular vote for the Democratic presidential candidate. Column 1 presents the bivariate relationship between policy mood and election outcome. If the hype one sometimes hears were true—that state contests in the electoral college were wholly different from the national popular vote—then we would not know what to expect of these relationships. If, in the alternative case, the state contests were fifty small variations on the national contest, then the national estimates from Table 5.1 should emerge in the state-by-state data in similar form. They do. The bivariate effect of mood on outcome is estimated at 0.48, roughly the same as the (0.42) national aggregate effect. But the state-by-state estimate is highly significant, the simple result of having 517 cases to explain instead of a mere eleven.[10]

TABLE 5.2 Democratic Percentage of the Two-Party Presidential Vote: State by State, 1956–1996

Variable	*(1)* *Mood* *Alone*	*(2)* *Party and* *Incumbency* *Added*	*(3)* *Party, Incumbency,* *and Home State* *Added*
Policy mood[a]	0.48	0.87	0.87
	(0.10)	(0.10)	(0.09)
Incumbency[b]		5.54	5.54
		(0.52)	(0.51)
Democratic macropartisanship[c]		0.26	0.26
		(0.12)	(0.12)
Home-state advantage[d]			5.84
			(1.72)
Intercept	17.74	–20.70	–20.70
	(6.32)	(9.90)	(9.80)
R^2	.04	.27	.28
R^2 (adjusted)	.04	.26	.28
N	517	517	517

[a] Biennial estimate: The value for the election year and the preceding (odd-numbered) year is used.

[b] Effects dummy: Coded 1 if Democratic incumbent, –1 if Republican incumbent, 0 otherwise.

[c] Democratic percentage of national (two-party) party identification.

[d] Coded 1 if Democratic candidate from state, –1 if Republican from state, 0 otherwise.

As before, we model the state outcome as a function of national macropartisanship, a variable like mood that varies over time but is constant across states, and the same incumbency dummy as before. Here (see column 2 of Table 5.2) the estimates begin to take on a more robust character. The estimated impact of mood strengthens to 0.87 and the other two coefficients take on expected and highly significant values. We now predict (1) that each one-point movement in national mood in the liberal direction produces a 0.87 percent Democratic gain in each state, (2) that a one-point gain in (national) Democratic macropartisanship produces a 0.26 percent Democratic election outcome gain, and (3) that incumbent presidents seeking a new term get a 5.54 percent bonus.[11]

One last wrinkle is added in column 3. There I model the favorite-son effect, the expected vote bonus in the single state claimed as "home" by each candidate (Lewis-Beck and Rice 1990). My motive here is simply to clean up the specification a bit, to assign that home-state variation where it properly belongs and not force other variables to try to account for it. Too pat to count as interesting, it simply helps to model such well-known effects as that of the favorite son to avoid misunderstanding a one- or two-time swing (such as Minnesota votes for Hubert Humphrey or Walter Mondale) as a permanent tendency. Modeling the unusual and exceptional helps get the usual and normal right. The effect of adding a dummy for the home state of the candidate is unremarkable; a modest improvement in fit is achieved without disturbing any of the other coefficients.

Dealing with State Variation

So far we have treated the states as independent cases for testing national effects. But the states do differ among themselves, at least in their partisan tendencies. Everything equal, we do not expect the same outcome from Massachusetts, for example, as from Utah. And although state measures of mood don't exist—in only a handful do requisite survey data over a lengthy period exist—we can gain some control over unwanted state-level variation by estimating pooled regression models in which each state is allowed to have its own natural level of election outcomes. This is accomplished by introducing a dummy variable (a variable that is scored 1 if the case is the appropriate state, 0 otherwise) for each state so that each state time series can start off from its own level. Although the estimates of state effects would have some substantive interest if our focus were state politics, here the purpose is simply to prevent state differences from interfering with the proper estimation of the other relationships. The advantage of this approach is that we don't force states that are politically different to be equal in the model. The disadvantage is that adding so many variables to a regression model is inefficient.

There are cases in which failure to model these unit effects biases other coefficient estimates. This is *not* one of those cases. That bias requires a variable in the pooled regression model to have cross-sectional variation, and none does here. But nonetheless we underestimate how well a time-serial effect works when we ask it to explain, for example, why Massachusetts and Utah are *always* different. Fitting a model, called least squares with dummy variables (LSDV), with separate intercepts for each state deals with that issue.[12] It forces the model to account only for change between elections (e.g., why is Utah more Republican in 1980 than in 1964?) rather than differences between states.

Accounting for state differences helps. Allowing each state to have its own intercept effectively removes between-state variation from the problem. A reestimated effect of mood alone on outcome is unaffected, except by its still smaller standard error from the better model fit. To the full model of the last table we add one more term in column 2 in Table 5.3. The evident partisan change of the American South in response to the

TABLE 5.3   Democratic Percentage of the Two-Party Presidential Vote in the States: LSDV and GLSE Models

Variable	(1) Mood and State Intercepts	(2) Full Model with State Intercepts	(3) Full Model: GLS Error Components
Policy mood[a]	0.48	0.81	0.86
	(0.09)	(0.08)	(0.10)
South (interaction)[b]		−8.61	−2.11
		(1.78)	(0.99)
Democratic		0.27	0.26
macropartisanship[c]		(0.10)	(0.12)
Incumbency[d]		5.62	5.56
		(0.42)	(0.51)
Home-State Advantage[e]		−1.34	−0.07
		(1.50)	(1.74)
Intercept(s)	(not shown)	(not shown)	−19.71
			(9.91)
R^2	.30	.55	.27
R^2 (adjusted)	.23	.50	.27
N	517	517	517

[a] Biennial estimate: The value for the election year and the preceding (odd-numbered) year is used.
[b] Scored 1 for 1964–1996 for ten states of the ICPSR southern code, 0 otherwise.
[c] Democratic percentage of national (two-party) party identification.
[d] Effects dummy: Coded 1 if Democratic incumbent, −1 if Republican incumbent, 0 otherwise.
[e] Coded 1 if Democratic candidate from state, −1 if Republican from state, 0 otherwise.

civil rights revolution of the early 1960s (often elaborated, my own account is Carmines and Stimson 1989) is now modeled as an intervention, an effect that first occurs in 1964 and then continues for all subsequent elections.[13] This captures the fact that the South can't simply be modeled as more or less Democratic than the nation; it is more Democratic before 1964 and less so after. As model specification improves, the estimated effect of mood on outcomes gets slightly stronger.

Column 3 of Table 5.3 is the last and best specification of a full model. A generalized least squares error components (GLSE) model, it is the same as column 2 except that the state effects are specified in the error term, where the expected autocorrelation from it ($\rho = .32$) is modeled in lieu of those forty-seven state intercepts. GLSE provides the control over state effects in the earlier model without the necessity of estimating all those additional coefficients. Its slightly lesser fit, R^2 is .27 as opposed to

.55 for the LSDV model, is actually relatively better, not purchased with the extravagant use of dummy variables.

The bottom line is that mood is a strong influence on election outcomes in the states as it is for the whole nation. But unlike the national result, the state results are highly robust. The coefficient that matters just doesn't vary much; all reasonably complete models produce estimates in the range of 0.80 to 0.90.[14] That is not true simply of the models I have chosen to report. All the alternate specifications I have considered but not reported are the same.

To get a view of why the estimated effect of mood on presidential outcome is so robust, I display the bar graph of simple presidential outcomes seen before, this time eliminating the estimated effects of macropartisanship and incumbency from Table 5.3. What remains is all that is not successfully predicted by these two variables. What is quite clear from Figure 5.3 is that mood is strongly associated with these residual outcomes, moving closely with the presidential outcome, once the other effects are under control.

Despite the strong estimated effect of mood on presidential elections, I don't wish to claim much understanding. For if some of the effects are as simple as more liberal policy preferences leading to more Democratic votes, I doubt that all are so simple. The demonstration is a daunting task,

FIGURE 5.3   Residual Presidential Vote and Mood

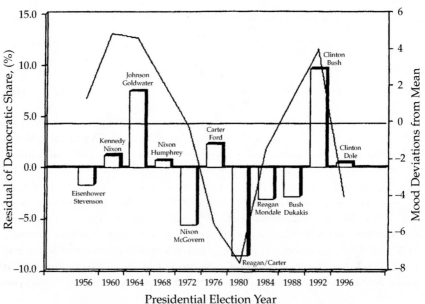

but I would expect to see more subtle, maybe more interesting, facets of mood at work in electoral politics. It may well influence what campaigns look like, what policy positions informed candidates chose to take or resist, what they choose to emphasize or downplay. These things matter, for they affect what elections come to mean. This is a theme to which I will return after a similar look at elections for Congress.

Congressional Elections

Congressional elections are tougher to explain. With policy considerations secondary, joined with candidates who are free to position themselves with little constraint, our expectation for the effect of mood is far from steady. Public opinion in this situation might matter and yet leave no evidence that it does. Where presidential candidates are too well known to control the policy image they project, members of Congress and their challengers are less known, more free to maneuver. It would be a fine service to political science for them to offer a fixed target so the changing mood could raise or lower candidates' prospects, but one suspects that rational candidates would rather shift with the tides of opinion than simplify political research. Just as boats shift with the tide and ride neither higher nor lower because of it, candidates who position themselves relative to the mood of the moment will vitiate evidence of it.

It is even worse than that. Pairs of candidates representing the two major parties do not take their parties' mean positions in each contest. If the Democrats are usually more liberal and the Republicans more conservative, it is with respect to the distribution of opinion within the district, not the nation.

The two houses of Congress are elected with different structures. Accordingly we take them up separately, starting with the lower house.

The House of Representatives

The expected effect of the more complicated and diffuse competition between candidate pairs is a lesser impact of mood on voting in House of Representatives contests than in the presidential case. And that is in fact the case. It is so much the case that with the small sample of *national* election data, no significant relationship is observed. The estimated effect of mood on outcome comes close, p = .055, but does not achieve significance at the standard level. If we were to stop here, we would have to do so with the conclusion that the effect in question had failed to be demonstrated.

But House election outcomes may equally well be represented as seats won and lost, the constitutional translation of votes. Here, in column 2 of Table 5.4, we see a somewhat different story. Seats are *not* merely votes translated into a different metric. The translation is nonlinear. Factors that

TABLE 5.4   Elections for the House of Representatives: Votes and Seats

Variable	Votes %	Seats #
Policy mood	0.12	2.05
	(0.07)	(0.61)
Democratic	0.58	5.74
macropartisanship	(0.12)	(1.04)
Midterm drop-off effect	–2.42	–14.06
	(0.53)	(4.72)
Intercept	12.06	–202.29
	(8.82)	(79.09)
R^2	.69	.67
N	23	23

move vote totals in seats that are safe for one of the parties translate into nothing, whereas those that matter at the margin in closely contested cases have a heavy influence. Although we don't know enough about these differences to specify how outcomes might differ between votes and seats, we do know enough not to be surprised when they turn out to differ. And that is what we see here. The almost significant mood effect in the votes model is quite highly significant in the parallel model predicting seats. Here each one-point movement toward liberalism in mood translates into a two-seat gain for the Democrats. That produces a total swing of about 24 seats between the extreme cases of mood, which is a notable proportion of the seats that actually change hands.

The Senate

Clearly a parallel sort of problem to explain from a theoretical point of view, the U.S. Senate presents practical differences in data that require a bit different approach from the one to the House. Much thinner than the House, with about thirty-three races per year instead of 435, the Senate data have one advantage over the House data—that states are meaningful and continuous electoral units—and one disadvantage—that the six-year periodicity of Senate elections doesn't allow continuous state time series of election results.

As a practical matter, Senate election results are much noisier data. Not a statewide average of several contests, they are a single contest where the outcome may swing wildly on one or two factors, such as whether incumbents seek reelection and whether the opposition mounts a serious or token challenge. This more erratic behavior makes statistical modeling more difficult at the level of individual states and contests.

For a first look we see in Figure 5.4 the Senate outcomes in percentage of Democratic seats[15] and, as always, domestic policy mood.

The figure has a simple interpretation. Policy mood is a striking predictor of Senate election outcomes. The two run pretty much in tandem. When they don't, even the discrepancies are just what an elections analyst would expect. Unpredicted Democratic success in 1974 and 1976 would be expected as a residue of the Watergate scandal, which so tainted the Republican party. Having nothing to do with policy or ideology, the scandal would have been predicted (and was before the fact) to help Democratic candidates do better than otherwise expected.

The same apparent pattern seen in the figure is captured in regressions of Democratic wins on mood and other predictors (see Table 5.5). Even mood all by itself is a fair predictor, the coefficient showing that every one-point movement in mood translates into a 1.02 percent Democratic gain. The Senate outcomes vary over a range from 33 percent (eleven of thirty-three in 1980) to 79 percent (twenty-six of thirty-three in 1964) Democratic victories. Of that forty-six point range, mood accounts for about twelve (1.02 times the twelve-point movement in the range of mood). In terms of practical politics, a one-point movement in mood is worth one seat in the U.S. Senate.

FIGURE 5.4   Liberal Moods and Democratic Wins in the U.S. Senate

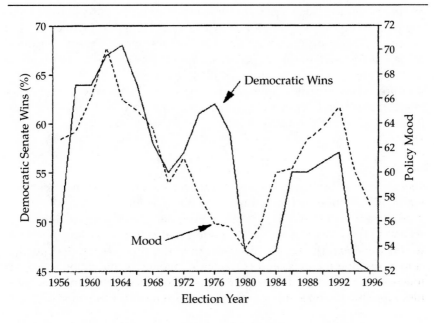

TABLE 5.5   Elections for the U.S. Senate: Democratic Seats

Variable	Democratic seats
Policy mood	1.02
	(0.17)
Democratic	1.60
macropartisanship	(0.26)
Intercept	−98.16
	(19.68)
R^2	.76
N	23

Responsiveness: The evidence we have just seen supports the conclusion that elections for the U.S. Senate are more responsive to public preferences than are those of the House of Representatives. A unit change in mood, that is, produces a higher percentage turnover of Senate seats than House seats. It does not follow, however, that the Senate is more responsive to public opinion than is the House. This result says only that Senate *elections* show more opinion influence than House elections.

What else is there? What this result does not speak to is the degree to which the behaviors of Senators and House members respond to changes in public opinion, *independent of elections*. And this point is not idle speculation, for we now know from a related research program (Stimson, MacKuen, and Erikson 1995) that this is precisely the case. Outcomes in the House respond strongly to changes in public opinion while they are happening; they do not await the next election result. Senate outcomes are less responsive in this direct sense; they are more likely to drift away from public opinion until corrected by an election result. The two bodies thus are very different in how they respond to public opinion. But the net effect, the degree to which what they do is in accord with what the public wants, is about the same.

Mood and Mandates

One of the oldest ideas about electoral politics, the notion of an election mandate—elections sending a message about voter preferences for what government should do—has taken a drubbing from voting and elections scholars. The naive appeal of the notion that elections mean something was battered on the shoals of voter ignorance, inattention, and apathy, confounded by the dismissal of personal ideology from voting behavior, replaced to a significant degree by the related idea of "realignment," and unhinged by a notion of retrospection, which has backward-looking voters sending messages about performance and past, not policy and future. If voting-behavior scholarship were the Wild West, mandate would have been tarred and feathered, ridden out of town on a rail.

And yet, the idea slips back from time to time. Not in every election, not even every presidential election, but from time to time, those who try to fathom the meaning of American politics look at elections and pronounce mandates. Neither a small nor academic matter, these pronouncements are important because they are self-fulfilling. Belief in mandate is requisite for the thing itself. Deprive 1933 (the New Deal), 1965 (the Great Society), 1981 (the Reagan revolution), or 1994 (the "Republican Revolution") of widespread belief by political actors that they had witnessed mandates in preceding elections and one would be hard-pressed to account for bursts of massive policy change in institutional settings that always before successfully resisted them.

Mandates and Survey Research

Voting-behavior scholars look at the behavior of individuals, try to observe change, and apportion it into effects caused by stable or changing partisanship, candidate preferences, and policy attitudes. They[16] find that attitudes toward candidates matter a lot and that other sorts of attitudes are of smaller import, often mixed and confused. But the standard voter survey is a weak research design when it comes to the mandate issue. It can tell us how much voters know or don't know, the balance of their policy preferences, and so forth. But it is not at all good at assessing change.[17] Its timing—just before and just after elections—limits observation to a brief and surely atypical moment. And it cannot control the leakage of individual attitudes causing, changing, reinforcing, and undermining one another. The conceptual order of analyses, where some attitudes are called "party," others are called "candidates," and others "issues," is imposed by the analysts. For the voter there are just "attitudes," and there is every reason to believe that each influences every other.

If mandates were big and obvious, such designs might find them. And even then the analysts would have to suspend disbelief a bit, for the results could never be unambiguous. Mandates with a more subtle character would not be seen. Effects would be there, at the margin, but they could not be so decisive in this weak design to overcome skepticism. But electoral mandate could be—has been, I will assert—of great importance without being big and obvious.

What would it take to produce a mandate? By definition it would take a shift of voter policy preferences expressed in electoral outcomes. But electoral outcomes vary a good deal for reasons other than mandate, and so just any shift expressed in any outcome wouldn't necessarily be powerful evidence. Shift of preference and outcome could be coincidence, could be of magnitude too small for a meaningful message. The landslides often attending reelection bids of incumbent presidents, for example, need to be discounted as evidence to some degree. The matter is not as simple as measuring the size of the vote swing.

With but a handful of cases for analysis, a truly rigorous operational definition of the phenomenon is probably beyond reach. A "requisites of mandate," like the common "requisites of realignment," would probably be a pseudoscientific tailoring to known historical cases. It seems more honest—at least less silly—to pick the cases first and let the reader decide than to tailor an operational definition that will then select the cases "objectively."

Three Elections, Three Messages

The cases I wish to consider mandate elections, 1964, 1980, and 1994, will come as no surprise. Analysts at the time thought voters spoke their convictions (although of course they have thought that about other elections that seem more dubious cases). They produced remarkable consequences for government. The 1964 and 1980 cases represent high points, liberal and conservative, respectively, of policy mood. The 1964 case is also the high point of Democratic presidential outcomes, an astounding ten points better than the second best. The 1980 case is not the best Republican year; in percentage terms the reelection victories of 1956, 1972, and 1984 are larger. It counts nonetheless as a dramatic victory, breaking the hold of an incumbent seeking a second term. If we discount the effect of incumbency, 1964 would easily still be the best Democratic victory whereas 1980 would become the best Republican showing.

But elections say more than which candidate for president won or lost. We see messages too in congressional results. Where the presidential contest is confused by the personal attractiveness of two competing candidates, hard to disentangle from all the other reasons for winning or losing, congressional—and particularly House—contests tend to cancel out personal and idiosyncratic effects. When large numbers of candidates are swept in or out at the expense of the other party, we are inclined to posit national forces at work.

If we ask why it is that observers seem to see messages in some elections and not others, some plausible answers are mood itself, perhaps captured in the clarity and extremity of the policy positions of winning and losing candidates; the one-sidedness of the presidential contest;[18] House and Senate election outcomes; and movements in partisanship. For a summary view of these things, I zoom in on the three chosen contests and look at indicators of each component. Policy mood is the familiar measure. The presidential result is the percentage that is Democratic of the two-party vote. House and Senate outcomes are net seat changes on election day.[19] Partisanship is the Democratic proportion of the two-party identifiers.

Because each measure has a different metric, they are presented in Figure 5.5 as ratios to the most extreme values in the series. By definition, then, measures take on a value of 100.0 for their most extreme liberal or Democratic year, −100.0 for the most extreme conservative or Republican years, and ratio values in between when the year in question is not most extreme.

The figure conveys a clear message about 1964. It is the most liberal year of the eleven presidential contests on mood,[20] the most Democratic presidential vote, the largest Democratic seat gain in the House, the largest Democratic seat gain in the Senate,[21] one of (but not the) largest gains in Democratic partisanship. All this is in the context of an election between a very liberal Lyndon Johnson and the most conservative Republican (to that time) of the New Deal era. I am hard-pressed to think of evidence that might have added to the case for a liberal mandate.

The 1980 election is almost as strong in the Republican and conservative direction. The most conservative mood was matched to the most

FIGURE 5.5   Five Components of Electoral Mandates for 1964, 1980, and 1994

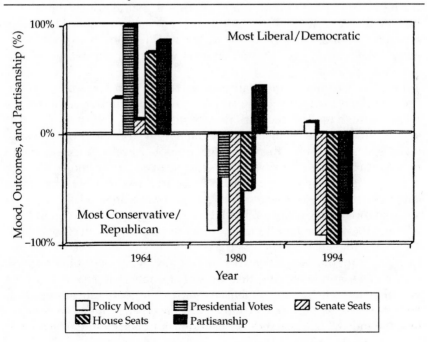

Republican of both House and Senate outcomes, the latter particularly dramatic in numbers and in producing change of party control. The presidential vote was well on the Republican side of normal but, up against incumbency, not most extreme. Republican gains in partisanship in 1980 were modest; the harvest of the Reagan era coming four years later. And again the candidates presented ideological choice. Carter, moderate to liberal by historical Democratic standards, probably was perceived to be left of what he truly was. Reagan, on the other hand, presented no ambiguity. Along with Goldwater from the earlier contest, Reagan presented a new standard for the meaning of conservatism. The dramatic reversal in Senate contests was of the same character, the big and unexpected Democratic losses were of well-known liberals at the hands of visibly conservative challengers mounting highly ideological campaigns.

The "Republican Revolution" election of 1994 presents us with a rarity of American politics: a midterm election widely believed to carry an important policy message. The most dramatic event of that year was the largest Republican seat gain in the House for the period—and (not shown in the figure), the first Republican majority in the House in forty years. Senate turnover was almost as dramatic, failing to garner equal attention largely because Republican majorities in the Senate had occurred in the 1980s. Partisanship shows a strong swing in the Republican direction. The one anomaly for 1994 is our concept of central interest: mood. Here what the measure in the figure does not capture is that although the level of mood is about normal for the period, its change since its 1992 liberal high is among the most striking in the series. Its direction, that is, was strikingly conservative, even though its level was about normal for modern American politics.

This is what the commentators saw when they declared mandates. Political scientists focused instead on individual attitudes and behavior, reaching more modest conclusions. Abramson et al. (1983), for example, showed that the 1980 Reagan victory came from an electorate that was on balance closer to Carter than to Reagan in policy preferences.[22] Evidence of the clear personal preference of Reagan over Carter and of strongly negative retrospective evaluations of the Carter presidency complete the case against mandate. These findings are not to be doubted. They are the careful work of fine scholars. But all are limited by the focus on individuals and the concomitant design inability to observe the effects of change. The individual analysis shows an electorate mostly closer to Carter than Reagan in the months of fall 1980. The aggregate over-time analysis shows an electorate moving steadily and strongly in Reagan's conservative direction. The net movement over a decade was quite strong. After 1974 it was unbroken, every year more conservative than the previous one. "Mandate" is a macro-level concept. "Elections" and "electorates" send messages. Individual voters too may communicate policy content in their votes. But they always do so to some degree, and they always speak contrary to one another, on both sides of real policy debates. Mandates arise from the net preference of one side over the other, and that is a system-level property.

What the mandate idea has lacked all along is an unambiguous measure of the purported message. Election results can be close or one-sided, mixed or decisive. But without knowledge of a preference message that might be expressed in votes, we have no electoral evidence that cannot be dismissed as the result of other factors. Policy mood is such a measure of message. Married to election outcomes, it suggests clear-cut evidence that occasional elections in the modern era send messages from the governed to the governors.

I turn last to a more speculative look at the future, giving in to the temptation to ask, What is the mood of the moment and where is it taking us?

NOTES

1. This, however, is a much easier case. All survey houses are trying to measure the same thing when they ask partisanship questions. The very high correlations between scale and individual series and, in particular, the .985 correlation with the most numerous, the Gallup series, suggest both great measurement reliability and that we needn't have worked so hard to get an optimal measure; Gallup would have done fine.

2. In the first edition of this book, I observed an apparent weak relationship but suggested that it might not survive better evidence. That is what has occurred; eight additional data points succeeded in demonstrating that the relationship was not really there.

3. The simple statistical evidence is mixed. A product moment correlation of .36 suggests a connection. But with $N = 11$ that correlation is less than the requisite for the customary .05 significance level.

4. The 1980 contest was a three-candidate affair. Carter, the incumbent president, received only 42.4 percent of the total vote. And the Democrats captured but 49 of 538 electoral votes and lost their long-time control of the U.S. Senate. In terms of what one might reasonably have expected, given party strength and incumbency, it was the worst Democratic showing since the beginning of the New Deal.

5. The t statistic for mood is 1.87, just short of the .05 critical level of 1.94, with 6 degrees of freedom. In a similar model (not reported), with mood paired with incumbency, it is easily significant, with $t = 2.44$.

6. The quotes indicate a certain tongue-in-cheek skepticism about calling this model fully specified. There are other variables that reasonable theories would suggest as candidates. But with only eleven cases, a three-variable model is about as far as one can go without starting to tailor variables to particular data points.

7. The 1976 contest is a difficult coding decision. Gerald Ford was the incumbent president, to be sure, but not having been elected, except in his Michigan congressional district, his incumbency status was dubious. I have coded 1976 a nonincumbent election. The results to be presented are affected by this decision, but the effect results mainly in a trade-off of explanatory power between incumbency and party, leaving mood little changed.

8. The variable is coded in such a way as to be always positively associated with Democratic voting, no matter whether that party is in or out of power.

9. Alaska and Hawaii lack results before statehood, and the Alabama contest of 1964 did not provide voters an opportunity to vote for Lyndon Johnson, the national Democratic candidate. These three states hence do not appear in analyses exploiting the regular, pooled data structure.

10. The goodness-of-fit contrast between national and state is what one would expect from sample size. R^2 is higher (.13 to .08) with the small sample, where capitalization on chance is unavoidable. But adjusting for degrees of freedom lost, which reduces the small sample fit to a trivial .01, has no effect at all on the large sample estimate. The fit here nonetheless does not suggest confidence that the bivariate specification is correct, which indeed it is not.

11. Disposable income, a variable that does not appear in the model, merits some comment. This all-purpose, elections-predicting and -forecasting champion, when added to the model, produces evidence that it may be given more credit than it deserves. Specifically, disposable income invariably fails to be statistically significant in specifications that include mood. Without mood in the model, it performs as expected. With mood present it drops out. The two variables are highly collinear, with $r = .58$ ($N = 9$). Mood always dominates disposable income in a statistical sense; when they compete to predict outcomes, mood is always highly significant and barely diminished whereas the income coefficient goes to zero. If they are accidentally related, this suggests that income may be a good election-outcomes predictor because it is spuriously related to policy mood (never before measured). But they may not be accidentally related. Durr (1993a) explicitly postulates a causal scenario in which greater relative prosperity causes policy liberalism. These results must be classed as suggestive only, because they are based upon such a small number of independent measures.

12. I deal with the technical side of pooled regression models in Stimson 1985, where the theory, terminology, and application of pooled dummy variables (LSDV) and error components (GLSE) models are treated in detail. My interpretation in the text can be understood without technical background.

13. The effect is a permanent shift, but that cannot be modeled with such a short time series, particularly when the one-time effect of 1964 is so dramatic that it must decay. The heart of the "solid South" for Kennedy and Johnson in 1960, the states of the Deep South totally rejected the Democratic ticket of 1964, the effect not greatly different in Alabama (where Johnson was not even on the ballot) from neighboring states (where he might as well not have been).

14. In other analyses, not reported, where states that cause problems for one or another reason are deleted, the estimate rises into the 0.45 range.

15. The variable is number of Democratic winners over number of seats with elections. This proves better behaved as a national aggregate than alternatives such

as percentage Democratic of the national vote for Senate. Because the same states are not contested in successive elections, which states are contested influences the national popular vote as a function of state size and the state's Democratic or Republican tendencies.

16. Perhaps I should use *we*, for I have contributed to this literature, and the thrust of my own contributions is very like the mainstream I here call into question.

17. And 1964, one of the two most interesting cases, cannot usefully be addressed with the Michigan surveys because a wholesale changeover in issue measurement technology that year obviates the measurement of change in issue preference.

18. Mandates would not have to be limited to presidential contests, but we seem unwilling to find the grand messages in midterm contests—even very one-sided ones—that we draw from the presidential contest. Some midterms that suggest mandates would be 1958, 1966, 1974, and 1978, the partisan direction of each consistent with policy mood. Each also forecasts victory for the opposition in presidential elections to come, suggestive evidence that the outcomes are more than just an adjustment to the previous presidential election.

19. Using outcomes as total seats won (instead of changing hands) produces nearly identical outcomes.

20. The measure here, a four-year change in mood, seems unimpressive, a result of the fact that the change is computed from a year that is itself almost the most liberal on record.

21. In the case of the Senate, the "large" seat gain is a mere two seats, tying the best Democratic performance thus measured in presidential years. What that number fails to show is that the Democrats reelected the best Senate class on record (1958) and even added two seats on top of that. If the measure were numbers of seats held, 1964 would still mark the best Democratic year—and 1980 the worst.

22. Indeed, their analysis employed many of the same National Election Study policy preference items that make their way into the estimates of policy mood.

6

Reflections on the Present and Future of American Politics

In the previous chapters we have seen public opinion as concept and as measure, a way of thinking about what the public wants and a way of putting concrete numbers onto a scale. Here we turn more to practical questions, such as how we should understand the opinion of the moment and where we go from here. Before we begin, we need to take stock of what we know about public opinion now, some of which is what we have learned about public mood since the original edition of this book.

Here I set out models of both government response to opinion and opinion response to government. Then I turn to the politics of the 1990s and beyond.

A Model of Opinion Response

To get a handle on the present and future—to make sense of this meandering mood—it is useful to have a self-conscious formulation of the dynamics of government response to the electorate and vice versa. We need to ask, "What moves policy activity in Washington?" and "How then does the electorate respond?" My story builds heavily upon two recent publications [my own work with Erikson and MacKuen (Stimson, Erikson, and MacKuen 1995) and Chris Wlezien's model of public as thermostat (Wlezien 1995)] and anticipates a third, forthcoming volume [Erikson, MacKuen, and Stimson (n.d.)]. I begin with a summary statement of the dynamic representation thesis and then look at how the electorate responds to what government does.

Government Response to the Electorate:
Dynamic Representation

The classic story of representation, enshrined in Democratic theory and embedded in the U.S. Constitution, uses elections to enforce public opinion on government. Primarily a retrospective account, the standard thesis is that government acts in one period of time, and then, following that, the electorate decides to reward or punish incumbents for faithfully following its preferences or not. The result of electoral choice is that the mix of personnel in government is altered—more in line with the electorate—in the period subsequent to the election.

This "electoral connection" story works best with incumbents who either (a) don't desire reelection—freeing them to violate the electorate's preferences—or (b) aren't smart enough to guess right what they ought to have been doing—they get out of touch because they didn't correctly discern what their constituents wanted from them. Neither of these conditions looks much like American politics as we know it. American politicians do typically behave as if they cared a good deal about reelection. And professionals are pretty good at sensing what the public wants and where it is going.

If this is the case, then another route to representation is "rational anticipation," wherein savvy politicians sense how the public's views are evolving in "real time," anticipate how those views might come into play in *future* elections, and modify their positions strategically. In the full story, with both "electoral connection" and "rational anticipation" modes in play, public opinion has a dual impact. It has an indirect influence through past elections on the ideological composition of government. And then it has a direct influence, as politicians sense it and change their positions on the fly.

What we now know from a test of this setup (Stimson, MacKuen, and Erikson 1995) is that the evidence for dynamic responsiveness of government to electoral preferences is very strong. All branches of American government (the president, both houses of Congress, and the Supreme Court) respond positively to changes in public opinion. The three elected branches respond quite vigorously. Each moves strongly—with no dampening at all between the size of the public opinion signal and the policy response—and quickly, with most of the response in place within a year. The first part of the dynamic now established, we turn to the second: how citizens respond to policy change.

Electorate Response to Government

I begin the statement of public response to policy change with a statement that is alternately self-evident and controversial, namely, that the

American public is moderate. It is self-evident because it is a mathematical necessity that the summary center of *any* distribution must be moderate relative to the distribution. It is controversial because it flies in the face of a long history of political rhetoric, where advocates for both left and right claim that their position is the "real" center of American politics. Such advocates necessarily reject the evidence of public opinion surveys, which has never been kind to either left or right visions of the "true" public. I am a respecter of evidence, and the evidence shows moderation.

If we ask what this moderate electorate sees when it sees government in action, the answer would be that it sees two clusters of politicians: Democrats generally to its left, Republicans generally to its right.[1] We presume reactions to policies actually in force—in effect, those of the party currently in power. The moderate electorate alternately experiences "too left" policies from one party and "too right" from the other. Presented with choices that ask for more or less government involvement in a variety of issues, it naturally tends to choose "more" the longer it has experienced the "less government" policies of the right and to choose "less" the longer it has experienced the "more government" policies of the left. As the parties constantly miss the center in their policies, the electorate constantly pulls back in that direction.

The moderate electorate as a result produces a negative feedback, always moving left when government moves right and moving right when government moves left. In the short run that creates tension for government not to stray too far from the middle. In the long run the countermovement of public opinion enhances the likelihood of cyclical change of government, with parties alternating in power, neither ever able to hold on to it for lengthy periods. And by mixing regimes of left and right over time, public opinion produces the cyclical moderation—as an average over time—that the electorate cannot achieve in a single election.

This mode of public opinion error correction works for the whole span of our analysis. Here I illustrate how it looks for the politics of the 1990s.

On Revolutions, Contracts, and Normal Politics:
Public Opinion in the 1990s

The first edition of this book, written in late 1990, included in the final chapter a section titled, "The Unnoticed Liberalism of Current American Politics." There I noted the obvious fact that public opinion in America— as tapped by the mood indicator—was moving strongly toward liberalism and had been since Ronald Reagan's election triumph of 1980. It was "unnoticed," because the political commentary of the time stressed conservatism as the dominant theme of American politics. While the book was being readied for publication, the United States fought and won the Gulf War, leaving George Bush with a spectacular standing in public esteem, more approval even than his popular predecessor.

In that context, where Reagan-Bush conservatism had been ascendant since 1980 and where the public seemed to have certified it in Bush's approval rating, it was awkward to assert growing liberalism. In that light the most serious problem for my story of public mood was that the story was violently out of step with the consensus of the times. It was natural to argue, and some did, that any measure that led to conclusions "everyone knew" were wrong must have had some equally unnoticed problem in its construction. Republican electoral dominance in 1980, 1984, and 1988, coupled with Bush's apparent lock on 1992, were awkward facts. The last particularly had to undermine faith in a measure that had moved steadily in the direction of a political party, the Democrats, that could not win the presidency.

The Economy and Public Mood in 1992

George Bush looked so strong for a few months that the early word on 1992 was that Democratic defeat was so foreordained that no serious candidate would emerge to challenge Bush. But then Bush's standing began a dramatic erosion that would not stop until Bill Clinton defeated him in the November 1992 election. The conventional interpretation of the 1992 result—indeed almost the only interpretation—is that it resulted from a sour American economy that left voters ready for change, any change. There is much truth in that story; it can be seen, for example, in consumer expectations for the future that were plumbing new depths before election day.

But there are some discordant notes as well. The 1992 contest was a disaster for presidential election forecasters, most of whom were heavily reliant upon economic indicators as forecasting tools. The problem is that the objective indicators showed an economy not all that bad.[2] Year-to-year changes were consistently positive, pointing, if not to a strong economy, then to one that appeared headed in the right direction. What was in those indicators that voters did not see? Or what did voters see that was not in the indicators? Clearly the answer to this query is that voters rejected George Bush's stewardship. It was not just that things were (relatively) bad; there was a belief that they would not get better under Bush's leadership. As much as voters revered Bush's foreign policy leadership, they had concluded that he would not produce a strong domestic economy. That is how we square the consumer pessimism at the time with indicators that were moderately good.

This is where the drift of public opinion toward liberalism plays an electoral role. As I argued in the previous chapter, there is no simple translation of mood into voting intention—nothing like, "I am now left of center, I should vote Democratic this year." Things are much more subtle. The story I would tell of 1992—and the reader is warned that speculation is coming—is that voters most of all distrusted Bush's economic *policy*. As the economy stumbled, and stumbled again, Bush repeatedly said, in essence, "Do nothing; it will correct itself."[3] This was simple economic conservatism, a Bush variation on Ronald Reagan's popular assertion that "government *is* the problem." But an activist—which is to say, liberal—public did not want to hear conservative solutions in 1992. It preferred Bill Clinton's "take charge" activism. Twelve years of movement toward liberalism provided a constituency that wanted to hear candidate Clinton talk about putting the government to the problem of moving the economy forward.

One can argue a simple "blame the incumbents for hard times" story of 1992. But that story doesn't square well with an electorate that had decided during the 1980s that the Republican Party was generally better at managing the economy than were the Democrats. An electorate that believed in conservative approaches would have given Bush another chance to prove himself. This one didn't.

The Clinton First Term

Bill Clinton assumed the presidency with weak public support and failed to recover it. His first two years got generally unfavorable commentaries. Commentators on foreign policy, for example, were so skeptical about Clinton that his policies were routinely declared to be failures before they were tried. On the domestic front, he followed a two-pronged approach, dealing with the deficit through tax increases and implementing health-care reform. The tax increase, passed on a party-line vote, was initially harmful to Democrats (but would come to look positive in the long term, as wonderful developments in the domestic economy eventually gave a positive hue to Clinton economic management). The failed health-care initiative exposed Clinton to embarrassment from the perception of inept handling and seemed to melt his "New Democrat" claims of moderation into his opponents' picture of big government liberalism.

Public opinion, which had reached a liberal peak before Clinton's 1992 election, marched steadily back toward conservatism during Clinton's first two years (see Figure 6.1). As Clinton acted, first on tax increases and then on health care, the strong support for activist government melted away. And it happened fast. About half of the increases in liberal sentiment that were the product of twelve years of conservative government disappeared in the first twenty-four months of the Clinton administration. The movement of policy mood in those twenty-four months was sharply and steadily back toward conservatism.

FIGURE 6.1   Mood in the Clinton First Term

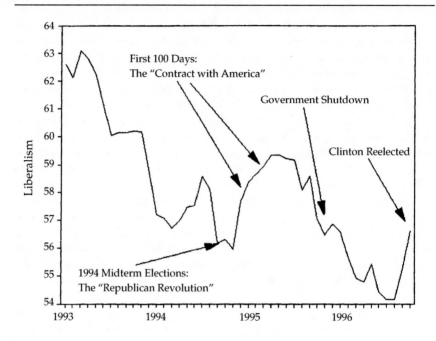

The Republican Revolution

Movement toward conservatism anticipated the 1994 midterm elections and quite probably contributed to the size of the "Republican Revolution" that resulted. Republican victories in all sorts of contests, but most particularly in the House of Representatives, seemed then a change of near earthquake proportions. Deliberately nationalized by Republican leadership with its "Contract with America," the election outcome was widely interpreted as a ringing endorsement of conservative principles and a personal repudiation of Bill Clinton. That the Clinton White House joined in this morning-after spin gave it added credence.

It seems an almost inevitable fact of political life that sweeping election victories are over-interpreted. Professionals who should know better see marginal change and declare that the political world is forever altered. And so we did in the aftermath of the 1994 elections. A clean party victory that probably indeed carried some message became instead a "revolution." The message of Figure 6.1 is the usual one: voters preferred a more moderate course than they were getting from the Clinton administration. Note that the mood indicator, down some seven points from the strong liberalism that elected Bill Clinton, is still nonetheless liberal.

While voting for the party that would declare a "revolution," 56 out of 100 voters preferred on balance more government to less!

No such moderation was seen on election night 1994 or in the months that followed. Republicans instead set out first to establish a record by passing the entire Contract in the first 100 days. Given that Contract items were pretested on public opinion and known to be popular, that should have worked reasonably well. But the Republican leadership moved far beyond the Contract in attempting genuinely daring reductions in government. Unlike Ronald Reagan, who talked budget cutting but didn't actually do much of it, the Gingrich Republicans set out to pass what had previously been known as the Kasich budget—a full-scale assault on government. A mix of proposals that would actually save billions of dollars, such as revisions to the expensive Medicare and Medicaid programs and to others that had more to do with ideology than money (eliminating the National Endowment for the Humanities and public broadcasting subsidies), the Kasich budget actually made hard cuts, the kind that hurt.

Old hands in government have always known that the public always supports budget cutting as rhetoric but rarely supports the real thing. This is where talk of "revolution" became troublesome. The Republicans would never have run an election campaign in which they promised massive cuts in popular programs such as Medicare/Medicaid. But having effected a "revolution"—which truly drew support from moderate and noncontroversial elements—they proceeded to implement policies that had never drawn public support. Gingrich's First 100 Days confronted American voters with sharp attacks on environmental regulation, with elimination of a highly popular public television system, with proposals to end SEC regulation of financial markets, and on and on—all of these attacks were leveled at government programs that had been instigated with voter approval and remained highly popular. Newt Gingrich's public assertion that a return to orphanages might be a good alternative to welfare programs for single mothers managed to build some support for even the least popular element of government spending.

It was an amazing time. But there was nothing amazing about the public response. It was, as always, a moderate rejection of extreme proposals. The 104th Congress managed the unintentional result of reminding voters of why many "big government" programs were popular: they did things that ordinary people cared about. Public policy mood began a move back to the liberal side.

Gingrich, in public statements in April 1995, said that Congress would demand that Clinton go along with its budget and would bring the government to a halt if he did not do so. When Gingrich Republicans made good on that threat several months later (the mechanism a refusal to pass a "continuing resolution" that would have enabled the government to function while budget negotiations continued), no attempt to blame the

White House looked credible, and the Republican Congress found itself blamed by an angry public. That ended the revolution. From that point onward Republican leadership moved to moderation and accommodation with Clinton to win back some of the esteem it had lost in such a short time. With the end of dramatic proposals came a stop in the opinion movement toward liberalism. Bill Clinton was undoubtedly the beneficiary of the "Republican Revolution." In trouble in 1994, his liberal programs came to seem less threatening than those of his conservative opponents. From the dramatic moment of the shutdowns through election day 1996, Clinton's lead in the polls was never once threatened.

Symbols vs. Substance: Ideological Confusion

To make sense of the events of 1994 and 1995—the public mandate for conservatism swiftly withdrawn in the face of real conservative policy[4]—we must once again return to the conundrum of symbolic conservatism and operational liberalism. It is a strange public that sets off a "revolution" and then wants to hang the revolutionaries within weeks of taking power. Part of the explanation for this quick change of heart I have already given: the mandate was much smaller than the Republican response. But that doesn't explain all of it.

What happened when the Republicans set out to implement their revolution is also explicable from our understanding that support for conservatism does not imply support for conservative policies. Almost a contradiction in terms, it is nonetheless the case that millions of Americans who proudly style themselves "conservatives"—and prove it by voting for conservative candidates—nonetheless prefer more government to less.[5] They did what we would expect. These millions of voters like conservative talk and dislike conservative action. They approved of the former and added their votes to the "revolution." They disapproved of the latter and swiftly turned on the conservative Congress they had helped elect.

We never seem to get ahead of this contradiction between symbol and substance. Commentaries on American politics seem so caught up in rhetorical excess, in painting a picture of the "true" electorate either left or right, that we don't acknowledge the contradiction, that it is *both* left and right: left in policy substance, right in political symbols. Since this appears to have been the case now for some decades, there is no reason to think that this pattern will soon disappear.

The Future

Public opinion, it is now clear, responds to what government does. Thus an understanding of its future course necessarily is conditional on a prediction of what future governments will do. We can predict with some confidence that opinion will continue on its moderate course, reacting against policies of both left and right. But we can't have much confidence about what those policies will be.

The politics of the 1990s is more ideological and more imbued with partisan hostility than has been the norm of earlier decades. A consequence of this, perhaps, is that public opinion has seemed to react both more quickly and more strongly than it did in earlier decades. More moderate and more peaceful conditions of the past produced public response that was itself more gradual. Responses that took many months, or even years, in the 1950s and 1960s, seemed to express themselves almost in days in the 1990s.

That makes forecasting the future particularly difficult. The pace of change in the 1990s is so fast that a change of course before this volume is published is possible. With considerable fear of being wrong, I venture two speculations about the public opinion of the near term, both tending in the liberal direction.

Economic Security: Durr (1993b) argues that collective goods come to be more valued when individual goods are secure. This predicts support for expansion of government activities at times when most citizens are confident about personal economic security. Citizens who prefer a society characterized by high levels of equality and concern for the least fortunate might nonetheless find the cost of these collective goods—taxes—too high to bear when they are in doubt about the economic security of themselves and their families. But given a high level of satisfaction and security in personal goals, the fruit of prosperity, such citizens would feel freer to spend for social goals. That predicts rising liberalism of opinion in times of sustained economic growth and stability. The American economy, seven years into a period of economic recovery and growth as I write, is now producing that personal economic security and satisfaction. "Security" is more than good economic numbers; it is good economic numbers repeated over such a lengthy period that people begin to forget the doubts of the past. It is new generations who come of age without ever having known the fear and gloom of bad times. With but a single recession in the sixteen year span after 1982, we must now be close to such a condition.

No More Collar: In the first edition of this book I noted the impact on American opinion of what I called "The Fiscal Collar": the state of permanent government deficits that stifled discussion—theretofore common in American politics—of *new* government programs and activities. When we, as a nation, could not pay for the current level of government activities, we lost interest in the agenda of government-expanding activities. The deficit forced a continuing public discussion of the issue of cutting government spending. Although cuts in the end were quite small, relative to the talk of cuts, perhaps the more important impact of this decade and a half of budget concern was that we lost interest in even thinking about expanding the government role, whereas "How much to expand?" was the question that had dominated earlier decades.

I write in the year when the first balanced budget of a lifetime for many citizens is in prospect. The genie of expanding government, still well within the bottle, seems likely to emerge in the longer run. When we get used to the idea that the United States federal government can actually afford all of the activities it undertakes—and we haven't yet—it seems all but inevitable that we will again begin to dream up new things it might do to make life better for its citizens. "There ought to be a law," someone will say. And we will pass that law, and we will enforce it. Then the story begins anew, not with "The End," but with yet another cycle.

Notes

1. This is not a necessary truth, for we can imagine a politics much like we experienced in the 1950s, when both party groups were so close to the center, and so diverse within themselves, that a perceptive electorate might have experienced both as moderate. But the politics of the last four decades has witnessed quite dramatic ideological polarization of the party system. Those who were mismatched to their party (generally southern conservatives among Democrats and liberals on the Republican side) have changed parties or left politics.

2. And we now know that the recovery that would eventually be credited to Bill Clinton had already started in the third quarter of 1992, when the numbers on growth and prosperity started an upward movement still unbroken as I write in 1998. The 1992 third quarter numbers, released before the election, suggested recovery in progress but were apparently discounted by voters who had already decided against Bush. This is not surprising since two previous "recoveries" had failed to be sustained, and a single quarter's indicators were not enough to document a trend.

3. And in fairness to historical fact, he was quite probably right. The economy was moving on a positive course without activist intervention from the White House.

4. To call the acts of the Gingrich House of Representatives "policy" is a bit of an overstatement. To be sure, the public was exposed to a lot of radical talk as the House moved on proposals that would have seemed well off the edge of the ideological map at other times. But the most radical acts of the 104th House failed to win support even in the Republican U.S. Senate, let alone from the Clinton White House, and did not become law.

5. See Erikson, MacKuen, and Stimson (n.d.) for an extensive analysis of this issue. There it is documented from individual level analysis that the modal preference of self-styled "conservatives" is for increased government spending on a

range of programs in the domains of education, race, cities, welfare, health, and the environment, each conventionally understood to be liberal. Although "conservatives" don't wish to spend as much as "moderates" or "liberals," they join both of those groups in wishing to increase programs, on balance, rather than cut them.

Appendix 1:
An Algorithm for Estimating Mood

To deal with the vexing missing-value issue, it is useful to switch focus from what we don't know, the missing values, to what we do know. We do have pieces of information for each survey question measured more than once over time about the *relative* values it takes when it is measured. If, for example, the liberalism index is higher in some period t than in some previous period $t–k$, then (excepting the usual problem of sampling errors) we have some basis for believing that period t is more liberal than $t–k$. And if the pattern recurs across samples, then sampling error can be ruled out as explanation.

Backward Recursion

We still wouldn't know anything about missing periods, and the information is now issue-specific. But presume we give the final index (at period t) some arbitrary value, say 100. We then have a basis for deriving a value for $t–k$. Because we can know the ratio of t to $t–k$ and we have a value for t (100) then Issue$_i$ at $t–k$ must be: Issue$_{i,t–k}$ = 100 * (Issue$_{i,t}$/Issue$_{i,t–k}$).

Now, because every issue measured at t has the same arbitrary value (by definition) and values of previous periods are ratios of that one value, then the metric in which all issues are measured is comparable. Comparable metric permits averaging across issues to find a central tendency if one exists. If there were no central tendency then we would be averaging across issues, some too high, some too low, where the result would be expected to cancel and leave only small random fluctuations as a summary score for each period. If there are central tendencies, issues as a group would be high or low on average for particular periods, and averaging would not cancel out that systematic effect.

This procedure leaves us (1) with only those issues that happen to be measured in the final period under analysis, and subsequently (2) estimates of the latent underlying mood only for those earlier periods in which members of that particular set of issues are available. But we can proceed further, for we now have an additional piece of information, the *estimated* value of mood in some earlier period, say $t–1$ the product of the first step. Thus we can recursively repeat this step, using *t*–1 as a base for comparison. Some issues measured at *t*–1 will be those already considered (because they were also measured at *t*) and some will be additions. Both new and old will be reestimated backwards in time with the new information about *t*–1. The recursion is repeated until all issues have contributed to the estimation and information about all time points has been exhausted.

Ultimately, every issue available for period *t* contributes its ratio with all other available periods to the summary scale value for *t*. No missing information enters into the calculation at any point.

$$Mood_t = \frac{\sum_{i=1}^{n} \sum_{j=1}^{t} \frac{Issue_{ij}}{Issue_{ib}} * Metric_b}{n} \qquad [\text{A.1}]$$

where
$I = 1, n$ is all available issues for period *t*
$J = 1, t$ is all available dyadic comparisons for issue *i*
b is the base period for the recursive metric generation
$Metric_b$ is the value of the metric for period *b*.

What's going on in the dyadic algorithm is mainly averaging. The only novelties to the process are that the averaging process first works out a common metric and then averages only the measured values, not the more numerous missing ones. Without missing values, the process produces a weighted average. But without missing values this whole process would be an easy matter. Because of them there is an added bit of challenge.

Forward Recursion

All this logic works equally well, but not identically, starting from arbitrary values for the first period and working forward through time. The same ratios get used in both cases, but forward and backward recursions differ in the numbers of times that particular ratios enter into the calculation, and thus implicitly in the weight they exert on the solution. The two estimates, backward and forward, are thus correlated but different estimates of the same concept. This difference is exploited to make possible the measurement of scale reliability, the correlation of the two methods.

Smoothing

Because the raw data input into estimation is aggregated survey data, we begin with the knowledge that it will be influenced by sampling error. For any particular survey reading we know that it will contain sampling error, but we do not know how much or in which direction. For a *series* of such readings, a smooth underlying phenomenon—when captured in survey marginals—will show a zigzag pattern over time. The series will approximate the underlying phenomenon but add on random up-and-down movements caused by sampling fluctuation in the estimates. We can't know that the particular peaks and valleys of the pattern we see are actually errors, but we do know that deviation from smoothness is to be expected.

Averaging over numerous items, where that is possible, eliminates most of the noise induced by sampling fluctuation. Items from different samples will contain different errors. Because these errors are random, they will tend to cancel one another, producing a smooth average series. But where numerous items are unavailable, the zigzag of sampling fluctuation remains. We introduce exponential smoothing to deal with this issue. The rationale is that one wishes to observe common movements in the evolution of issue series and not tailor a fit to particular zigs and zags that may be random variation around a deterministic process. Smoothing is particularly appropriate with survey marginals, which are known to contain random fluctuation from sampling.

The exponential smoothing model is:

$$y_t = \alpha x_t + (1 - \alpha)x_{t-1}$$

where y is the smoothed version of x. The intuition is that if the past (x_{t-1}) provides any useful information for predicting y_t, then some portion of the variation in x_t is a deviation from the smooth path of x. This is seen in zigzag behavior, where the series tends to return to normal levels after extreme movements away from them.

The α parameter is estimated by minimizing within sample forecast error. Thus it is fully determined by the data. Exponential smoothing has the desirable property that it will not over-smooth. If the data are already smooth, a situation that often occurs with annual aggregation levels, then α converges on 1.0 and $y_t = x_t$. Smoothing occurs in both forward and backward directions in time, the result of which is that the raw data series become exponentially weighted moving averages of past and future values.

Smoothing operates on the raw series during estimation. That means, in effect, that the smoothed value is presumed to be a better measure of the true level of the series than is the original, and that it is the ratios of the smoothed values to past and future (smoothed) values of the series that drive the ultimate measure. The impact of smoothing varies in direct proportion to the apparent randomness of the series. Where the original series are highly patterned, the impact of smoothing is rarely discernable.

Where, in contrast, they exhibit a good deal of period-to-period zigzag fluctuation, the effect of smoothing is large.

The first-cut estimate of mood is now simply the average of smoothed forward and backward estimates. But which issues should be used? That presents a quandary. What goes in has something to do with what comes out. That presents hard choices. Some issue preference measures seem closely tied in theory and evidence to the idea of mood. Others, for example, foreign policy "internationalism," seem remote. And there are many in between. It is desirable that the analyst not have too large a role in the outcome by issue selection. And yet throwing everything into the pot can overwhelm the measure with unrelated patterns and noise. Given that the issues that contribute their dyadic variance to mood are likely to vary in their association with the latent concept and that it is undesirable to wholly discard numerous issues because their associations are small, the procedure can be modified by including a weighting term u^2, which taps the communality of the issue-mood association as in factor analysis. The communality may be estimated by correlating estimated mood with each of the issues. The squared bivariate correlations then become communality estimates for [A.2].

$$Mood_t = \frac{\sum\limits_{i=1}^{n} \sum\limits_{j=1}^{t} u_i^2 * \dfrac{Issue_{ij}}{Issue_{ib}} * Metric_b}{n} \qquad [A.2]$$

where the equation is the same as [A.1] except weighted by u_i^2, an estimate of the common variance of $Issue_i$ and Mood.

This presents the usual circularity problem, the same issue as in using estimated communalities in factor analysis. You must make an assumption about the communality of each item (in this case that $u_i^2 = 1.0$; each item is a perfectly valid indicator of mood). From this assumption and the given data the underlying scale may be estimated. Then it is possible to *estimate* the communality. If the assumption had been correct, then the estimate would be the same as the assumed value—confirmation that all is correct. In the general case, however, the initial assumption will not be correct, inducing a small error in the estimated scale. This is then observed in the discrepancy between assumed and estimated communalities. Because the scale estimate is not particularly sensitive to this one assumption, the resulting estimate will be good but imperfect. The whole process can then be repeated, this time starting with the "good" estimate as the new assumption. On the next round there will be a new, but smaller, discrepancy between assumption and estimate. The process then continues in this fashion, until the discrepancy between assumed and estimated communalities for every item is effectively zero (i.e., <.001). This is the solution.

Additional Dimensions

Extraction of the first dimension from the data series now permits re-analysis of the possibility of a second. First items are transformed, one at a time, into residuals of a regression of the item series on the first dimension. An arbitrary constant is added to each value to move item ranges away from zero, where the use of ratios becomes too sensitive. Then the entire procedure is repeated to extract a second dimension. It could in principle be extended to further dimensions as well.

Scale Metric

The scale in which the latent mood dimension is measured is initially arbitrary—a function of the arbitrary 100 starting point. To increase the interpretability of the final product, as a last step the scale metric is transformed to match a weighted average of the means and standard deviations of the constituent items. Weighting is by the final estimates of commonality, so that each item contributes to the scale metric in the same proportion as its contribution to the scale.

Appendix 2: Selected Data Series

TABLE A.1   Alternative Estimators of Mood

	Regression Estimation	Dyadic Recursion Dimension 1	Dyadic Recursion Dimension2
1952		50.73	63.15
1953		54.90	64.54
1954		54.17	68.73
1955		58.56	69.20
1956	60.68	60.63	67.01
1957	69.17	61.20	63.23
1958	65.29	65.77	65.97
1959	70.23	65.50	64.00
1960	66.16	63.74	60.72
1961	65.49	70.06	64.00
1962	66.26	69.25	62.51
1963	68.16	66.65	60.52
1964	65.13	63.76	61.02
1965	59.84	61.72	60.91
1966	58.82	62.99	63.27
1967	59.73	63.53	61.98
1968	62.86	64.47	58.08
1969	62.24	59.72	58.37
1970	66.44	61.91	64.43
1971	69.38	61.96	67.49
1972	69.74	60.09	67.91
1973	64.93	58.80	66.27
1974	67.49	58.76	65.35
1975	63.39	56.73	64.97
1976	59.48	54.78	62.67
1977	59.61	54.02	61.33
1978	56.07	53.37	60.17
1979	59.42	52.46	58.82
1980	52.86	52.42	57.78
1981	53.72	53.78	57.40
1982	59.30	55.56	56.69
1983	60.97	59.01	58.32
1984	62.03	59.93	58.95
1985	61.89	59.50	59.11
1986	62.87	60.82	58.35
1987	61.73	62.10	59.22
1988	64.46	64.00	58.70

(continues)

TABLE A.1   *(continued)*

	Regression Estimation	*Dyadic Recursion Dimension 1*	*Dyadic Recursion Dimension2*
1989	67.37	65.85	57.43
1990	68.47	66.65	56.11
1991	69.22	66.31	55.69
1992	68.38	65.14	55.19
1993	61.31	63.68	52.91
1994	60.19	61.60	50.14
1995	59.72	64.35	50.03
1996	57.45	58.44	50.56

TABLE A.2   Five Welfare State Policy Estimates

	Education	*Health*	*Race*	*Urban Problems*	*Welfare*
1964		69.1	44.2		
1965		71.3	39.0	55.0	
1966		68.7	34.5	54.3	
1967		71.5	40.2	57.7	
1968	88.2	75.2	43.2	61.8	
1969	87.7	77.0	42.5	63.4	
1970	87.9	78.3	48.3	64.4	
1971	87.3	78.3	50.5	65.0	67.0
1972	87.4	78.4	47.0	63.8	67.8
1973	86.7	76.1	47.2	63.6	68.6
1974	87.2	76.9	46.0	63.3	70.7
1975	85.7	73.4	40.6	59.7	70.6
1976	85.5	72.4	39.9	58.3	62.1
1977	85.9	71.8	38.5	60.1	62.2
1978	85.7	70.6	38.1	58.6	61.7
1979	87.1	70.2	38.2	59.5	62.1
1980	86.1	68.9	39.6	58.0	63.4
1981	87.5	70.6	36.8	60.8	68.4
1982	88.7	72.0	42.4	61.3	71.1
1983	90.1	73.5	46.5	61.9	71.3
1984	90.5	72.5	50.3	64.8	74.0
1985	90.4	74.1	48.8	62.6	73.3
1986	91.4	77.1	51.3	61.7	74.9
1987	91.0	78.5	53.4	61.3	72.3
1988	92.4	79.4	55.4	65.5	74.3
1989	93.5	81.0	53.7	66.4	74.1
1990	93.9	81.4	56.0	67.9	76.6
1991	92.7	81.0	56.5	66.3	75.4
1992	93.3	83.2	57.9	66.3	64.6
1993	91.0	73.5	54.4	66.6	66.2
1994	91.1	69.8	51.8	67.5	62.7
1995	91.1	71.0	47.7	65.7	60.8
1996	91.2	72.2	52.2	64.9	60.4

TABLE A.3　Five Policy Estimates

	Size of Government (Figure 4.5)	*Crime, Liberties, and Guns (Figure 4.5)*	*Military Spending (Figure 4.5)*	*Environment (Figure 4.5)*	*Abortion Rights (Figure 4.8)*
1956	62.59	46.29			
1957	60.25	49.13			
1958	67.26	48.73			
1959	68.09	49.00			
1960	70.43	48.18			
1961	71.21	50.33			
1962	69.68	49.72			
1963	66.28	52.15			
1964	63.16	48.97			
1965	61.27	46.05			
1966	62.50	44.72			
1967	62.86	43.86			
1968	61.53	42.07			
1969	56.86	43.63	68.79		
1970	63.21	46.90	67.04		
1971	65.00	47.04	65.53	84.01	
1972	61.78	52.31	70.36	80.36	47.00
1973	60.79	51.76	60.66	74.82	53.91
1974	61.19	52.57	58.88	75.82	57.04
1975	59.28	49.73	54.10	72.82	55.66
1976	55.83	44.21	46.40	73.81	55.54
1977	55.71	43.18	39.98	71.63	55.71
1978	54.64	42.68	36.79	70.42	53.61
1979	54.48	44.44	34.51	67.32	55.90
1980	53.79	41.63	18.25	68.51	56.59
1981	55.22	39.52	24.92	74.47	55.97
1982	56.42	39.01	49.38	75.28	58.37
1983	59.65	41.31	57.89	80.87	55.24
1984	60.98	40.59	57.58	84.68	53.99
1985	60.31	38.84	63.53	83.26	53.45
1986	62.11	39.88	59.75	86.32	57.44
1987	63.01	40.63	57.54	88.31	54.94
1988	64.85	39.70	57.70	90.24	54.66
1989	65.48	39.44	63.05	90.74	57.11
1990	65.21	40.14	65.81	88.51	59.79
1991	65.24	42.93	56.02	86.05	60.66
1992	64.64	38.93	70.25	74.03	62.76
1993	61.51	41.49	71.44	79.84	61.25
1994	57.20	42.76	55.09	80.10	60.11
1995	54.53	47.85	55.09	79.50	62.72
1996	59.51	46.51	55.09	78.33	59.92

Appendix 3: Selected Domestic Policy Survey Questions

Items listed below are the subset identified in the text as "domestic policy" queries. These are the standard materials used to estimate mood. The subset includes the component series of Chapter 4, but excludes materials such as self-identified liberalism/conservatism and defense that are related to mood but not components of it. Series are identified by the originating survey house, but in some cases the associated dates will include use of the same question by other houses.

Gallup

1. Are you in favor of the death penalty for persons convicted of murder? [1953–1996]
2. Do you consider the amount of federal income tax which you have to pay as too high, about right, or too low? [1952–1996]
3. Do you think the _____ administration is pushing racial integration too fast, or not fast enough? [1962–1964]
4. In general, do you think the courts in this area deal too harshly or not harshly enough with criminals? [1965–1993]
5. In your opinion, which is more often to blame if a person is poor—lack of effort on his own part, or circumstances beyond his control? [1964–1990]
6. In general, do you approve or disapprove of labor unions? [1957–1986]
7. In some places in the United States it is not legal to supply birth control information. How do you feel about this—do you think birth control information should be available to anyone who wants it, or not? [1959–1968]
8. In your opinion, which of the following do you think will be the biggest threat to the country in the future—big business, big labor, or big government? [1965–1985]
9. Now here are some questions about guns. First, let's talk about handguns, such as pistols and revolvers. In general, do you feel

that the laws covering the sale of handguns should be made more strict, less strict, or kept as they are now? [1975–1988]

10. Would you favor or oppose having Alaska admitted as a state in the union? [1957–1958]

11. Would you favor or oppose having Hawaii admitted as a 49th state in the union? [1957–1958]

12. Would you favor or oppose a law which would require a person to obtain a police permit before he or she could buy a gun? [1959–1996]

13. Would you favor or oppose lowering the voting age limit so that persons 18, 19, and 20 years old could vote in elections? [1967–1970]

14. Some people say that government should give financial help to build schools, especially in poorer states. Others say this will mean higher taxes and that communities should build their own schools. Do you favor or oppose federal aid to help build new public schools? [1957–1961]

Harris

1. Do you favor or oppose a federal law requiring that all handguns people own be registered by federal authorities? [1971–1984]

2. Do you favor or oppose federal laws which control the sale of guns, such as making all persons register all gun purchases with federal authorities? [1975–1990]

American National Election Studies

1. In general, some people feel that the government in Washington should see to it that every person has a job and a good standard of living. Others think that the government should just let each person get ahead on his own. Have you been interested enough in this to favor one side over the other? Do you think that the government: [1964–1968]

2. Some people feel that the government in Washington should see to it that every person has a job and a good standard of living. Others think that the government should just let each person get ahead on his own. And of course other people have a position somewhere in between. Where would you place yourself on this scale, or haven't you thought very much about this? [1972–1996]

3. There is much discussion about the best way to deal with the problem of urban unrest and rioting. Some say it is more important to use all available force to maintain law and order—no matter what

results. Others say it is more important to correct the problems of poverty and unemployment that give rise to the disturbances. Where would you place yourself on this scale, or haven't you thought very much about this? [1970–1992]

4. There is much discussion about the best way to deal with racial problems. Some people think that achieving racial integration of schools is so important that it justifies busing children to schools out of their own neighborhoods. Others think that letting children go to their neighborhood schools is so important that they oppose busing. Where would you place yourself on this scale, or haven't you thought very much about this? [1972–1984]

5. Do you think that people in the government waste a lot of the money we pay in taxes, waste some of it, or don't waste very much of it? [1958–1992]

6. Some people say that Negroes should be allowed to live in any part of town they want to. How do you feel? Should Negroes be allowed to live in any part of town they want to or not? [1964–1976]

7. If Negroes are not getting fair treatment in jobs and housing, the government should see to it that they do. [1956–1960]

8. If the cities and towns around the country need help to build more schools, the government in Washington ought to give them the money they need. [1956–1962]

9. The government ought to see to it that every person who wants to work has a job. [1956–1960]

10. There is much concern about the rapid rise in medical and hospital costs. Some feel there should be a government insurance plan which would cover all medical and hospital expenses. Others feel that medical expenses should be paid by individuals, and through private insurance like Blue Cross. Where would you place yourself on this scale, or haven't you thought very much about this? [1970–1996]

11. The government ought to help people get doctors and hospital care at low cost. [1956–1962]

12. Some say the government in Washington ought to help people get doctors and hospital care at low cost; others say the government should not get into this. Have you been interested enough in this to favor one side over the other? What is your position? [1964–1968]

13. Some people think that the government should provide fewer services, even in areas such as health and education, in order to reduce spending. Other people feel that it is important for the government to provide many more services, even if it means an

increase in spending. Where would you place yourself on this scale, or haven't you thought very much about this? [1980–1996]

14. Some people are primarily concerned with doing everything possible to protect the rights of those accused of committing crimes. Others feel that it is more important to stop criminal activity even at the risk of reducing the rights of the accused. Where would you place yourself on this scale, or haven't you thought very much about this? [1970–1978]

15. Some people say that the government in Washington should see to it that white and Negro (black) children are allowed to go to the same schools. Others claim that this is not the government's business. Have you been concerned enough about this question to favor one side over the other? [1964–1986]

16. Some feel that if Negroes are not getting fair treatment in jobs the government in Washington ought to see to it that they do. Others feel that this is not the federal government's business. Have you had enough interest in this to favor one side over the other? [1964–1972]

17. Some people think the government in Washington should help towns and cities provide education for grade and high school children; others think that this should be handled by the states and local communities. Have you been interested enough in this to favor one side over the other? [1964–1968]

18. What is your feeling, do you think the government in Washington is getting too powerful or do you think the government has not gotten too strong? [1964–1992]

19. Some people feel that the government in Washington should make every possible effort to improve the social and economic position of Negroes and other minority groups. Others feel that the government should not make any special effort to help minorities because they should be expected to help themselves. Where would you place yourself on this scale, or haven't you thought very much about this? [1970–1996]

National Opinion Research Center

We are faced with many problems in this country, none of which can be solved easily or inexpensively. I'm going to name some of these problems, and for each one I'd like you to tell me whether you think we're spending too much money on it, too little money, or about the right amount. Are we spending too much, too little, or about the right amount on

1. . . . Solving the problems of the big cities? [1973–1996]
2. . . . Improving and protecting the nation's health? [1973–1996]

3. ... Welfare? [1973–1996]
4. ... Improving the conditions of blacks? [1973–1996]
5. ... Improving and protecting the environment? [1973–1996]
6. ... Improving the nation's education system? [1973–1996]
7. ... The environment? [1984–1996]
8. Do you consider the amount of federal income tax which you have to pay as too high, about right, or too low? [1976–1996]
9. Some people think that the government in Washington is trying to do too many things that should be left to individuals and private businesses. Others disagree and think that the government should do even more to solve our country's problems. Still others have opinions somewhere in between. Where would you place yourself on this scale, or haven't you made up your mind on this? (Respondents shown card with 1 to 5 scale on which point 1 indicates "I strongly agree that the government should do more" and point 5 indicates "I strongly agree that the government is doing too much." Point 3 indicates "I agree with both answers.") [1975–1996]
10. Some people think that the government in Washington should do everything possible to improve the standard of living of all poor Americans; they are at point 1 on this card. Other people think it is not the government's responsibility, and that each person should take care of himself; they are at point 5. Where would you place yourself on this scale, or haven't you made up your mind on this? [1975–1996]
11. Some people think (blacks/Negroes) have been discriminated against for so long that government has a special obligation to improve their living standards. Others believe that government should not be giving special treatment to (blacks/Negroes). Where would you place yourself on this scale, or haven't you made up your mind on this? [1983–1996]
12. Some people think that the government in Washington ought to reduce the income differences between the rich and the poor, perhaps by raising the taxes of wealthy families or by giving income assistance to the poor. Others think that the government should not concern itself with reducing this income difference between the rich and the poor. Here is a card with a scale from 1 to 7. Think of a score of 1 as meaning that the government ought to reduce the income differences between rich and poor, and a score of 7 meaning that the government should not concern itself with reducing income differences. What score between 1 and 7 comes closest to the way you feel? [1973–1996]
13. In general, some people think that it is the responsibility of the government in Washington to see to it that people have help in paying

for doctors and hospital bills. Others think that these matters are not the responsibility of the federal government and that people should take care of these things themselves. Where would you place yourself on this scale, or haven't you made up your mind on this? [1975–1996]

Opinion Research Corporation

1. In your opinion, which one of these do you think will be the biggest threat to the personal freedom of people in this country in the future? [1965–1974]
2. Many of our major central cities are experiencing financial difficulty, would you favor or oppose special federal aid for these central cities? [1976–1979]
3. Some people have said that instead of providing welfare and relief payments, the federal government should guarantee every American family a minimum yearly income of about $3,000. Would you personally favor or oppose such an income guarantee? [1969–1972]
4. There is a law that guarantees workers the right to form unions and bargain with their employers. On the whole, do you approve or disapprove of a law for this purpose? [1958–1965]
5. What is your feeling about government regulation of business— would you say it's better to regulate business pretty closely, or would you say the less regulation of business the better? [1962–1967]

Roper

We are faced with many problems in this country, none of which can be solved easily or inexpensively. I'm going to name some of these problems, and for each one I'd like you to tell me whether you think we're spending too much money on it, too little money, or about the right amount. Are we spending too much, too little, or about the right amount on

1. ... Welfare? [1971–1986]
2. ... Improving the nation's education system? [1971–1986]
3. ... Solving the problems of the big cities? [1971–1986]
4. ... Improving and protecting the nation's health? [1971–1986]
5. ... Improving and protecting the environment? [1971–1986]

There are many problems facing our nation today. But at certain times some things are more important than others, and need more attention from our federal government than others. I'd like to know for each of the things on this list whether you think it is something that the government should be making a major effort on now, or something the government should be making some effort on now, or something not needing any particular government effort now.

6. ... Trying to reform our income tax system? [1984–1986]
7. ... Trying to establish more controls to protect consumers on the products and services they buy? [1974–1987]
8. ... Taking steps to contain the cost of health care? [1979–1986]
9. ... Trying to solve the problems caused by ghettos, race and poverty? [1974–1987]
10. ... Trying to reduce unemployment? [1982–1987]
11. ... Seeking ways to protect the privacy of individuals in our society? [1974–1987]
12. ... Trying to slow down inflation in our economy? [1974–1987]
13. ... Taking steps to reduce the deficit? [1984–1987]

Trendex (General Electric)

I would like to get your opinion on several areas of important government activities. As I read each one, please tell me if you would like government to do more, do less, or do about the same as they have been on

1. ... Health measures? [1965–1982]
2. ... Improving Social Security benefits? [1978–1982]
3. ... Education? [1968–1982]
4. ... Expanding employment? [1966–1982]
5. ... Helping minority groups? [1966–1982]
6. ... On urban renewal? [1965–1982]
7. I notice you said you would like the government to do more on health measures. Would you favor this increased activity if it required an increase in taxes? [1972–1982]
8. I notice you said you would like the government to do more on education. Would you favor this increased activity if it required an increase in taxes? [1972–1982]
9. I notice you said you would like the government to do more on improving Social Security benefits. Would you favor this increased activity if it required an increase in taxes? [1978–1982]

Daniel Yankelovich

1. Do you favor or oppose each of the following ... Gun control laws? [1983–1984]
2. Do you favor or oppose mandatory registration of all handguns? [1977–1985]

References

Abramson, Paul R., John H. Aldrich, and David W. Rohde. 1983. *Change and Continuity in the 1980 Elections*, rev. ed. Washington, D.C.: CQ Press.

Adams, Greg D. 1997. Abortion: Evidence of Issue Evolution. *American Journal of Political Science* 41:718–737.

Barber, James David. 1965. *The Lawmakers: Recruitment And Adaptation to Legislative Life*. New Haven: Yale University Press.

Beck, Nathaniel. 1989. Estimating Dynamic Models Using Kalman Filtering. *Political Analysis* 1:121–156.

Beck, Paul Allen. 1986. Choice Context and Consequence: Beaten and Unbeaten Paths toward a Science of Politics. In H. Weisberg, ed., *Political Science: The Science of Politics*. New York: Agathon.

Bell, Daniel. 1960. *The End of Ideology*. New York: The Free Press of Glencoe.

Berelson, Bernard R., Paul F. Lazarsfeld, and William N. McPhee. 1954. *Voting: A Study of Opinion Formation in a Presidential Campaign*. Chicago: University of Chicago Press.

Bishop, George F., Alfred J. Tuchfarber, and Robert W. Oldendick. 1978. Change in the Structure of American Political Attitudes: The Nagging Question of Question Wording. *American Journal of Political Science* 22:250–269.

Braybrooke, David, and Charles Lindblom. 1963. *A Strategy of Decision*. New York: Free Press.

Campbell, Angus. 1960. Surge and Decline: A Study of Electoral Change. *Public Opinion Quarterly* 24:397–418.

Campbell, Angus, Philip Converse, Warren Miller, and Donald Stokes. 1960. *The American Voter*. New York: John Wiley & Son.

Cantril, Albert Hadley, with Mildred Strunk. 1951. *Public Opinion, 1935–1946*. Princeton: Princeton University Press.

Carmines, Edward G., and James A. Stimson. 1986. The Structure and Sequence of Issue Evolution. *American Political Science Review* 80:901–920.

_____. 1989. *Issue Evolution: Race and the Transformation of American Politics*. Princeton: Princeton University Press.

Conover, Pamela Johnston, and Stanley Feldman. 1981. The Origins and Meaning of Liberal/Conservative Self-Identifications. *American Journal of Political Science* 25:617–645.

Converse, Philip E. 1962. Information Flow and the Stability of Partisan Attitudes. *Public Opinion Quarterly* 26 (Winter):578–599.

_____. The Nature of Belief Systems in Mass Publics. In David E. Apter, ed., *Ideology and Discontent*. New York: Free Press.

_____ Popular Representation and the Distribution of Information. In James H. Kuklinski and John A. Ferejohn, eds., *Information and Democratic Processes*. Urbana: University of Illinois Press.

Converse, Philip E., Aage R. Clausen, and Warren E. Miller. 1965. Electoral Myth and Reality: The 1964 Election. *American Political Science Review* 59:321–334.

Dahl, Robert A. 1956. *A Preface to Democratic Theory*. Chicago: University of Chicago Press.

Davis, James A., and Tom W. Smith. 1980. Conservative Weather in a Liberalizing Climate: Change in Selected NORC General Social Survey Items, 1972–1978. *Social Forces* 58:1129–1156.

Durr, Robert H. 1993a. What Moves Public Opinion?: An Analysis of Changes in U.S. Domestic Policy Sentiment. Doctoral Dissertation, University of Iowa.

Durr, Robert H. 1993b. What Moves Policy Sentiment? *American Political Science Review* 87:158–170.

Engle, R., and M. Watson. 1981. A One Factor Multivariate Time Series Model of Metropolitan Wage Rates. *Journal of the American Statistical Association* 76:774–780.

Epstein, Lee, Thomas G. Walker, and William J. Dixon. 1989. The Supreme Court and Criminal Justice Disputes: A Neo-Institutional Perspective. *American Journal of Political Science* 33:825–841.

Erbring, Lutz. 1990. Individuals Writ Large: An Epilogue on the 'Ecological Fallacy' *Political Analysis* 1: 235–269.

Erikson, Robert S., Michael B. MacKuen, and James A. Stimson. *The Macro Polity*. New York: Cambridge University Press, forthcoming.

Eulau, Heinz, and John C. Wahlke. 1978. *The Politics of Representation*. Beverly Hills: Sage Publications.

Feldman, Stanley. 1990. Measuring Issue Preferences: The Problem of Response Instability. *Political Analysis* 1:25–60.

Fenno, Richard F., Jr. 1966. *The Power of the Purse*. Boston: Little, Brown.

_____. 1978. *Home Style: House Members in Their Districts*. Boston: Little, Brown.

Fiorina, Morris P. 1981. *Retrospective Voting in American National Elections*. New haven: Yale University Press.

Free, Lloyd A., and Hadley Cantril. 1967. *The Political Beliefs of Americans*. New Brunswick, N.J.: Rutgers University Press.

Freeman, John R., John T. Williams, and Tse-min Lin. 1989. Vector Autoregression and the Study of Politics. *American Journal of Political Science* 33:842–877.

Hamill, Ruth, Milton Lodge, and Frederick Blake. 1985. The Breadth, Depth, and Utility of Class, Partisan, and Ideological Schemata. *American Journal of Political Science* 29:850–870.

Hibbs, Douglas A. 1987. *The American Political Economy: Macroeconomics and Electoral Politics*. Cambridge, Mass.: Harvard University Press.

Jacobson, Gary C. 1987. *The Politics of Congressional Elections*. Boston: Little, Brown.

_____. 1990. *The Electoral Origins of Divided Government: Competition in U.S. House Elections, 1946–1988*. Boulder, Colo.: Westview Press.

Jacobson, Gary C., and Samuel Kernell. 1983. *Strategy and Choice in Congressional Elections, 2nd ed.* New Haven: Yale University Press.

Kingdon, John W. 1984. *Agendas, Alternatives, and Public Policies*. Boston: Little, Brown.

Kuhn, Thomas S. 1962. *The Structure of Scientific Revolutions*. Chicago: University of Chicago Press.

Levitin, Teresa E., and Warren E. Miller. 1979. Ideological Interpretations of Presidential Elections. *American Political Science Review* 73:751–771.

Lewis-Beck, Michael S., and Tom W. Rice. 1990. Localism in Presidential Elections: The Home State Advantage. In Douglas Madsen, Arthur Miller, and James A. Stimson, eds., *American Politics in the Heartland*. Dubuque, Iowa: Kendall-Hunt.

Lippmann, Walter. 1922. *Public Opinion*. New York: Macmillan.

MacKuen, Michael B., Robert S. Erikson, and James A. Stimson. 1988. On the Importance of Experience and Expectations for Political Evaluations. Paper delivered at the Annual Meeting of the American Political Science Association, The Washington Hilton, Washington, D.C., September 1–4, 1988.

Mayhew, David R. 1974. *Congress: The Electoral Connection*. New Haven: Yale University Press.

Niemi, Richard G., John Mueller, and Tom W. Smith. 1989. *Trends in Public Opinion: A Compendium of Survey Data*. Westport, Conn.: Greenwood Press.

Page, Benjamin I., and Robert Y. Shapiro. 1982. Changes in Americans' Policy Preferences, 1935–1979. *Public Opinion Quarterly* 46: 24–42.

_____. 1983. Effects of Public Opinion on Policy. *American Political Science Review* 77:175–190.

_____. 1992. *The Rational Public: Fifty Years of Trends in Americans' Policy Preferences*. Chicago: University of Chicago Press.

Page, Benjamin I., Robert Y. Shapiro, and Glenn Dempsey. 1987. What Moves Public Opinion? *American Political Science Review* 81:23–41.

Patterson, Kelly D., John T. Young, and Robert Y. Shapiro. 1986. Economic Status and Other Influences on Public Opinion Toward Social Welfare Policies. Presented at the 1986 annual meeting of the Northeastern Political Science Association, Boston, November 13–15, 1988.

Pitkin, Hanna F. 1967. *The Concept of Representation*. Berkeley: University of California Press.

Poole, Keith T., and Howard Rosenthal. 1985. A Spatial Model for Legislative Roll Call Analysis. *American Journal of Political Science* 29:357–384.

Robinson, John P., and John A. Fleishman. 1988. Ideological Identification: Trends and Interpretations of the Liberal-Conservative Balance. *Public Opinion Quarterly* 52:134–145.

Robinson, W. S. 1950. Ecological Correlations and the Behavior of Individuals. *American Sociological Review*. 15:351–357.

Scammon, Richard M., and Ben J. Wattenberg. 1970. *The Real Majority*. New York: Coward-McCann.

Schlesinger, Arthur M., Jr. 1986. *The Cycles of American History*. Boston: Houghton-Mifflin.

Schuman, Howard, and Stanley Presser. 1981. *Questions and Answers in Attitude Surveys: Experiments on Question Form, Wording, and Content*. New York: Academic Press.

Segal, Jeffrey A., and Albert D. Cover. 1989. Ideological Values and the Votes of Supreme Court Justices. *American Political Science Review* 83:557–565.

Shapiro, Robert Y., and John M. Gillroy. 1984a. The Polls: Regulation—Part I. *Public Opinion Quarterly* 48:531–542.

_____. 1984b. The Polls: Regulation—Part II. *Public Opinion Quarterly* 48:666–677.

Shapiro, Robert Y., and Kelly D. Patterson. 1986. The Dynamics of Public Opinion Toward Social Welfare Policy. Presented at the annual meeting of the American Political Science Association, Washington, D.C., August 28–31, 1986.

Shapiro, Robert Y., and Tom W. Smith. 1985. The Polls: Social Security. *Public Opinion Quarterly* 49:561–572.

Shapiro, Robert Y., and John M. Young. 1986. The Polls: Medical Care in the United States. *Public Opinion Quarterly* 50:418–428.

Shapiro, Robert Y., Kelly D. Patterson, Judith Russell, and John M. Young. 1987a. The Polls: Employment and Social Welfare. *Public Opinion Quarterly* 51:268–281.

_____. 1987b. The Polls: Public Assistance. *Public Opinion Quarterly* 51:120–130.

Smith, Tom W. 1981. General Liberalism and Social Change in Post World War II America: A Summary of Trends. *Social Indicators Research* 10:1–28.

Smith, Tom W. 1990. Liberal and Conservative Trends in the United States since World War II. *Public Opinion Quarterly* 54: 479–507.

Smith, Tom W., and Frederick D. Weil. 1990. Finding Public Opinion Data: A Guide to the Sources. *Public Opinion Quarterly* 54:609–626.

Stanley, Harold, and Richard Niemi. 1988. *Vital Statistics on American Politics.* Washington, D.C.: CQ Press.

Stimson, James A. 1985. Regression Models in Space and Time: A Statistical Essay. *American Journal of Political Science* 29: 914–947.

_____. Political Eras and Representation: Measuring Policy Mood. Presented at the annual meeting of the Political Methodology Society, Minneapolis, July 12–15, 1989.

_____. Political Eras and Representation: A First Analysis. Presented at the annual meeting of the American Political Science Association, Atlanta, August 31-September 3, 1989.

Stimson, James A., Michael B. MacKuen, and Robert S. Erikson. 1995. Dynamic Representation. *American Political Science Review* 89:543–565.

Stockman, David Alan. 1986. *The Triumph of Politics: How the Reagan Revolution Failed.* New York: Harper & Row.

Stokes, Donald E. 1963. Spatial Models of Party Competition. *American Political Science Review* 57:368–377.

Sullivan, John L., James Piereson, and George E. Marcus. 1978. Ideological Constraint in the Mass Public: A Methodological Critique and Some New Findings. *American Journal of Political Science* 22:223–249.

Tufte, Edward R. 1978. *Political Control of the Economy.* Princeton: Princeton University Press.

_____. *The Visual Display of Quantitative Information.* Cheshire, Conn.: Graphics Press.

Weisberg, Herbert. 1986. Model Choice in Political Science. In H. Weisberg, ed., *Political Science: The Science of Politics.* New York: Agathon.

Wicker, Tom. 1968. *JFK and LBJ: The Influence of Personality Upon Politics.* Baltimore: William Morrow & Co.

Wlezien, Christopher. 1989. The Political Economy of the Budgetary System. Doctoral Dissertation, University of Iowa.

_____. 1995. The Public as Thermostat: Dynamics of Preferences for Spending. *American Journal of Political Science* 39:981–1000.

Wright, Gerald C., Jr., Robert S. Erikson, and John P. McIver. 1987. Public Opinion and Policy Liberalism in the American States. *American Journal of Political Science* 31:980–1001.

Zaller, John P. 1990. Bringing Converse Back In: Modeling Information Flow in Political Campaigns. *Political Analysis* 1: 181–234.

_____. 1992. *The Nature and Origins of Mass Opinion.* New York, Cambridge University Press.

Zaller, John P., and Stanley Feldman. 1988. Answering Questions vs. Revealing Preferences: A Simple Theory of the Survey Response. Paper prepared for the annual meeting of the Political Methodology Society, Los Angeles, July 15–18, 1988.

Index

Printed in the United States
56212LVS00003B/132

9 780813 368900